THE BEST JOKE BOOK EVER

THE BEST JOKE BOOK EVER

Hundreds of really
funny joke, one-liners,
limericks, puns,
and much much more!

Edited by Marcia Kamien

Platinum Press, LLC
2012

ISBN - 13 - 978 - 879582 - 76 - 7

Printed and bound in the United States of America

First Edition

987654321

CONTENTS

ONE LINERS

ONE LINERS

I wondered why the baseball kept getting larger. Then it hit me.

If you jumped off a bridge in Paris, you'd be in Seine.

When cannibals ate a missionary, they got a taste of religion.

In a democracy it's your vote that counts. In feudalism, it's your count that votes.

What do you call a fish with no eyes? A fsh.

The soldier who survived mustard gas and pepper spray is now a seasoned veteran.

Two hats were hanging on a hat rack. One said to the other, "You stay here. I'll go on a head."

If I agreed with you, we'd both be wrong.

I'm single because I was born that way.

The midget fortune teller who escaped from prison is a small medium at large.

Many people are alive only because it's illegal to shoot them.

Don't worry about your health. It will go away.

Live each day as if it were your last. One day, you'll get it right.

Married men live longer than single men, but married men are a lot more willing to die.

I almost had a psychic girlfriend, but she left me before we met.

The difference between a girlfriend and a wife: 45 pounds.

The difference between a boyfriend and a husband: 45 minutes.

If at first you don't succeed, skydiving is not for you.

Not only is there no God, but try finding a plumber on Sunday.

Nobody goes to that restaurant any more; it's too crowded.

That's not an optical illusion; it just looks like one.

Grandchildren are God's reward for not killing your children.

Mothers of teens know why animals eat their young.

Help a man when he is in trouble and he will remember you the next time he's in trouble.

Forgive your enemy, but remember the bastard's name.

A husband is someone who, after he takes the trash out, gives the impression that he just cleaned the entire house.

Forgive your enemies. It messes up their heads.

Don't pick a fight with an old man. If he's too old to fight, he'll just kill you.

War never determines who's right–only who's left.

You're never too old to learn something stupid.

Money can't buy happiness; but it's so much nicer to cry in a Bentley than on a bicycle.

Always borrow money from a pessimist. He won't expect it back.

You don't need a parachute to sky-dive ... you need it to sky-dive twice.

314 backwards spells PIE.

What turns without moving? Milk, when it turns sour.

What's the longest piece of furniture in the world? The multiplication table.

What kind of mistakes do ghosts make? Booboos.

Most women don't know where to look when they're eating a banana.

Think of how stupid the average person is, and realize that half of them are stupider than that.

If you are going to try cross-country skiing, start with a small country.

FROM SAM LEVENSON:

Lead us not into temptation. Just tell us where it is and we'll find it.

You must pay for your sins. If you've already paid, ignore this notice.

The reason grandparents and grandchildren get along so well is because they have a common enemy.

Somewhere on earth, every ten seconds, there is a woman giving birth. She must be found and stopped.

Love at first sight is easy to understand. It's when two people have been looking at each other for a lifetime that it becomes a miracle.

On my fifth birthday, Papa said to me: "Remember, son, if you ever need a helping hand, you'll find it on the end of your arm."

At a Hawaiian luau they eat with their fingers. I have a family at home exactly like that.

"Do you believe in reincarnation?"
"I eat it every day. It's called hash."

Warning: consumption of alcohol may lead you to believe you're invisible.

I saw a woman wearing a sweatshirt with GUESS on it. "Implants?" I said.

My grandpa started walking five miles a day when he was 60. Now he's 97 and we don't know where he is.

The difference between outlaws and in-laws is that outlaws are wanted.

The nice thing about dating a homeless woman is that you can drop her off anywhere.

Person one: Doctor, I really need help.
Person two: I'll say! This is a bank

Mommy, there's someone at the door collecting for the Old Folks Home. Should we give them Grandma?

I've often wanted to drown my troubles, but I can't get my wife to go swimming.

A golf club comes into a bar and asks for a martini. "I can't serve you," says the bartender. "You'll be driving later."

Marriage changes sex. Suddenly you're in bed with a relative.

A couple is in bed together. He says, "I'm about to make you the happiest woman in the world." She says, "I'll miss you."

Q: What do you call an intelligent, good-looking, rich, sensitive man? A: A rumor.

Vatican press release:
Be all women informed that lying in bed, naked, entangled with somebody and screaming, "Oh my God, oh my God!" will NOT be considered praying.

Jack and Dan are discussing modern morals. Dan says, "I didn't sleep with my wife before we got married, did you?" Replies Jack: "I'm not sure. What was her maiden name?"

A blonde calls United Airlines. "Can you tell me how long it takes to fly from San Francisco to New York City?" she says.
The agent says, "Just a minute."
"Thank you," the blonde says, and hangs up.

A man is recovering from surgery when the nurse comes in and asks how he is feeling."Not bad, but I didn't like the four letter word the doctor used in surgery." "What did he say?" asks the nurse.
"Oops!"

My wife got me to become religious. Until I married her, I didn't believe in Hell.

"Honey, what do you suppose the neighbors would think if I mowed the lawn naked?"
"That I married you for your money."

The graveside service had barely finished when there was a massive clap of thunder followed by a huge bolt of lightning .
The widow calmly said, "Well, he's there!"

The cop got out of his car and the kid who had been stopped for speeding rolled down his window.
"I've been waiting here all day for you," said the cop.
Replied the kid: "Yeah, well I got here as fast as I could."
When he stopped laughing, the cop sent the kid on his way. No ticket.

A woman looking through the case of frozen turkeys, to the store employee: "Do these turkeys get any bigger?"
The answer: "No, ma'am, they're dead."

Wherever you go, there you are. Your luggage is another story.

I'm in a bridge club. I jump next Tuesday.

COUNTRY WESTERN SONGS YOU MAY NOT KNOW

I Ain't Never Gone to Bed with an Ugly Woman, but I Sure Woke Up with a Few

It's Hard to Kiss the Lips that Chewed my Ass Out All Day Long

She's Lookin' Better with Every Beer

I'm So Miserable Without You, It's Almost Like You're Here

She Took My Ring and Gave Me the Finger

If the Phone Don't Ring, You'll Know it's Me

Wouldn't Take Her to the Dog Fight, 'Cause I'm Scared She Might Win

My Wife Run Off with My Best Friend and I Sure Do Miss Him

I've Missed You, But My Aim's Improvin'

Now That You're Gone and Food Has Replaced Sex in my Life, I Can't Even Get into My Own Pants

I Had the Six Inches You Love and It Was My Foldin' Money

What's got four legs and one arm? A Rotweiler.

Sex before marriage isn't so awful... unless it interferes with the ceremony.

He said: What have you been doing with all the grocery money I gave you?

She said: Turn sideways and look in the mirror.

He said: Let's go out and have some fun tonight.

She said: Okay, but if you get home before I do, leave the hallway light on.

She said: What do you mean by coming home half drunk?

He said: It's not my fault. I ran out of money.

He said: Since I first laid eyes on you, I've wanted to make love to you in the worst way.

She said: Well, you succeeded.

He said: Why don't you tell me when you have an orgasm?

She said: I would, but you're never there.

On the wall of a restaurant ladies' room: My husband follows me everywhere.

Written just below it: No, I don't.

Consumption of alcohol may cause you to thay shings like thish.

RODNEY DANGERFIELD AT HIS BEST

A girl phoned me the other day and said: "Come on over, there's nobody home." I went over. Nobody was home.

I was such an ugly baby, my mother never breastfed me. She told me that she only liked me as a friend.

I was so ugly, my mother had morning sickness ... AFTER I was born.

One day as I came home early from work, I saw a guy jogging naked. I said to him, "Hey buddy, why are you doing that?" He said, "Because you came home early."

I worked in a pet shop and people kept asking how big I'd get.

My father carries around the picture of the kid who came with the wallet.

I went to see my doctor. "Doctor, every morning when I get up and look in the mirror, I feel like throwing up. What's wrong with me?" He said, "I don't know, but your eyesight is perfect."

We were really poor. If I wasn't born a boy, I'd have had nothing to play with.

If a married man is walking alone in a forest and expresses an opinion without anyone around to hear him, is he still wrong?

Marriage advice: Don't marry a beautiful person. They may leave you. Of course, an ugly person might leave you, too; but in that case, who cares?

THINGS TO DO THAT WILL MAKE YOU SMILE
(although maybe not anyone else)

1. Any time anyone asks you to do anything, ask if they wants fries with that

2. In the office, skip down the hall instead of walking.

3. Sing along at the opera.

4. In a restaurant, order a diet water.

5. When the money comes out of the ATM, shout: "I won! I won!"

6. Specify that your drive-thru order is "to go."

7. Tell your children at dinner, "Due to the economy, we're going to have to let one of you go."

8. When leaving the zoo, start running toward the parking lot, yelling, "They're loose! They're loose!"

There will be only 49 contestants in the Miss Black America Contest this year because no one wants to wear the banner that says "IDAHO.'

A Jewish woman goes to her rabbi and says, "Sam and Dan are both in love with me. Who will be the lucky one?"

The rabbi answers: "Sam will marry you. Dan will be the lucky one."

The best contraceptive for old people is nudity.

Have you been to Wal-Mart lately? You have to be 300 pounds to get the automatic doors to open.

Do ten millipedes equal one centipede?

I was born to be a pessimist. My blood type is B-negative.

I bet you I could stop gambling.

All power corrupts. Absolute power is pretty neat, though.

If your feet smell and your nose runs, you're built upside down.

Red meat is not bad for you. Green fuzzy meat is bad for you.

Gargling is a good way to see if your throat leaks.

Gun control: use both hands.

Failure is not an option. It's bundled with your software.

My mind is like a steel trap - rusty and illegal in 37 states.

The only substitute for good manners is quick reflexes.

It's not who you know, it's whom you know.

A clean desk is the sign of a cluttered drawer.

Follow your dreams...except for that one where you're naked at work.

If #2 pencils are the most popular, are they still #2?

I used to be a lifeguard, but some blue kid got me fired.

Is Marx's tomb a Communist plot?

Photons have mass? I didn't even know they were Catholic.

I had amnesia once. Maybe twice.

Originality is the art of concealing your sources.

Teach a child to be polite and courteous, and when he grows up, he'll never be able to edge his car onto a busy highway.

Contents may have settled out of court.

Most nudists are people you don't really want to see naked.

Imitation is not the sincerest form of flattery. Stalking is.

Should crematoriums give discounts to burn victims?

If I want your opinion, I'll ask you to fill out the necessary forms.

Can a blind person feel blue?

If a man with no arms has a gun, is he armed?

Two wrongs are only the beginning.

I've been on so many blind dates, I should get a free dog.

I can't get enough minimalism.

I'm one bad relationship away from having 30 cats.

Am I ambivalent? Well, yes and no.

A fool and his money can throw one hell of a party.

The following statement is true. The preceding statement is false.

For every action, there is an equal and opposite criticism.

A conclusion is the place you got tired of thinking.

A man calls 911 and says, "I think my wife is dead." The operator asks why he thinks that. He says, "Well, the sex is the same, but the ironing is piling up."

My girlfriend thinks I'm a stalker. Well, she's not exactly my girlfriend yet.

Neighbor knocked on my door at 2 AM! Can you believe it? Lucky I was still up playing my bagpipes.

I was explaining to my wife last night that when you die and are reincarnated, you must come back as a different creature. She said she'd like to come back as a cow. I said, "You're obviously not listening."

The wife has been missing for a week now and the police said to prepare for the worst. So I've been to the thrift shop to get all her clothes back.

A wife says to her husband, "You're always pushing me around and talking behind my back!" He says, "What do you expect? You're in a wheelchair."

I was in bed with a blind girl last night and she said I had the biggest penis she had ever laid her hands on. I said, "You're pulling my leg."

Only Irish Coffee provides in a single glass all four essential food groups: alcohol, caffeine, sugar, and fat.

Santa Claus has the right idea. Visit people only once a year. -Victor Borge

Be careful about reading health books. You may die of a misprint. -Mark Twain

By all means, marry. If you get a good wife, you'll become happy. If you get a bad one, you'll become a philosopher. -Socrates

The secret of a good sermon is to have a good beginning and a good ending; and to have the two as close together as possible. -George Burns

I've never hated a man enough to give his diamonds back. -Zsa Zsa Gabor

A bartender is just a pharmacist with a limited inventory.

A committee is a life form with six or more legs and no brain.

If you always take time to smell the roses, sooner or later you'll inhale a bee.

Karaoke bars combine two of the nation's greatest evils: people who shouldn't drink with people who shouldn't sing.

It will be a great day when education is paid for and we see the military holding a bake sale to raise funds.

In case of the Rapture, this office will be empty. With the possible exception of the guy in accounting.

If you believe you can tell me what to think, I believe I can tell you where to go.

If we have a moment of silence in public schools, shouldn't we also have a moment of noise in Bible schools?

By the time I realized my parents were right, I had kids who didn't believe me.

Every day I beat my own previous record for number of consecutive days I've stayed alive.

Every time I walk into a singles' bar I can hear Mom's wise words: "Don't pick that up, you don't know where it's been."

Firefighting is like sex: size, equipment, and technique are all important.

Blessed are they who can laugh at themselves, for they will never cease to be amused.

Have you ever noticed how nothing is impossible for those who don't have to do it?

If Jesus were here today, there is one thing he wouldn't be: a Christian. -Mark Twain

Never get into an argument with a schizophrenic person and say, "Just who do you think you are?"

Never think that war, no matter how necessary, nor how justified, is not a crime.

Those who can make you believe absurdities can make you commit atrocities.

When you have eliminated the impossible, whatever remains, however improbably, must be the truth.

What 3 letters change a boy into a man? AGE.

Other than that, Mrs. Lincoln, how was the play?

Animal testing is futile! The animals always get nervous and give the wrong answers.

Censored? Our books aren't censored! If they were, I couldn't write _____ or xxxx.

If your fiancee is an existentialist, would you give her a disengagement ring?

Neurotics build castles in the air; psychotics live in them; and psychiatrists charge them rent.

In just two days from now, tomorrow will be yesterday.

Whatever hits the fan will not be distributed evenly.

When you work here, you can name your own salary. I call mine "Fred."

I found Jesus! He was in my car's trunk when I got back from Tijuana.

I love cooking with wine. Sometimes I even put it in the food.

Nobody is perfect. I am a nobody. Therefore, I am perfect.

It's not who wins or loses. It's who keeps score.

Colt is coming out with a new pistol in honor of our Senators and Congressmen. It will be called The Legislator.

It won't work and you can't fire it.

Imagine living with 3 wives in one compound and never leaving the house for five years.

It is now believed that Bin Laden called the U.S. Navy Seals himself.

Politicians and diapers have one thing in common. They both should be changed regularly; and for the same reason.

By the time a man is wise enough to watch his step, he's too old to go anywhere. –Billy Crystal

Don't worry about avoiding temptation. As you get older, it will avoid you. –Winston Churchill

I don't feel old. I don't feel anything until noon and then it's time for my nap. –Bob Hope

The advantage of exercising every day is so when you die, they'll say, "Well, he looks great, doesn't he?"

"Hey, baby, what's your sign?"
"DO NOT ENTER."

"I've been seeing spots in front of my eyes."
"Have you seen a doctor?"
"No, just spots."

I answered my doorbell this morning and there was a young man, who said, "I'm a Jehovah's Witness."

I said, "Come in and sit down. What do you want to talk about?"

"Beats the hell out of me," he said. "I've never gotten this far before."

A man is sitting on his patio with his wife. He says, "I love you."

She asks, "Is that you or the beer talking?"

He replies: "It's me... talking to the beer."

My wife dresses to kill. She cooks the same way.

You can't change a man... unless he's in diapers.

MORE GEORGE CARLIN GEMS

A house is just a place to keep your stuff, while you go out and get more stuff.

As soon as someone is identified as an unsung hero, he no longer is.

If it requires a uniform, it's a useless endeavor.

The reason I talk to myself is because I'm the only one whose answers I will accept.

Just when I discovered the meaning of life, they changed it.

If the Cincinnati Reds were really the first major league baseball team, who did they play?

No one knows what's next, but everyone does it.

If you live long enough, sooner or later, everyone you know has cancer.

By and large, language is a tool for concealing the truth.

Have you noticed that anyone driving slower than you is an idiot and anyone driving faster than you is a maniac?

They say you shouldn't say nothing about the dead unless it's good. He's dead. Good.

-Moms Mabley

Don't worry about what people think. They don't do it very often.

One snowman turns to another snowman and asks, "Is it just me, or do you smell carrots, too?"

Warning: if you don't pay your exorcist, you may find yourself repossessed.

Women don't need to make fools of men. Most of them are the do-it-yourself type.

If you think the way to a man's heart is through his stomach, you're aiming too high.

A woman drove me to drink ... and I didn't even have the decency to thank her!

The things that come to those who wait may well be the things left behind by those who got there first.

It's okay to let a fool kiss you but don't let a kiss fool you.

An egotist is a person more interested in himself than in me.

A transvestite is a man who likes to eat, drink, and be Mary.

An impotent loser is a man who can't even get his hopes up.

A joke is like sex. Neither is any good if you don't get it.

He who laughs last probably didn't get the joke.

When I read about the evils of drinking, I gave up reading. -Henny Youngman

Give a man a fish and he will eat for a day. Teach him how to fish, and he will sit in a boat and drink beer all day.

If nobody knows the trouble you've seen, you don't live in a small town.

An egotist in usually me-deep in conversation.

A tax collector has what it takes to take what you've got.

Man's inhumanity to man has led to prizefights, wars, and buffet suppers.

If you think children don't know the value of money, try giving one a nickel.

Living in the past is a lot of fun. Besides, it's cheaper.

Some people have tact; others tell the truth.

A perfect example of minority rule is a baby in the house.

One woman to another: I never repeat gossip... so listen very carefully now.

Consumption of alcohol is a major factor in dancing like an idiot.

Some minds are like concrete–all mixed up and permanently set.

About the time a man gets his temper under control, he goes out and plays golf again.

No matter how bad a child is, he's still good for an exemption on your income tax return.

Some people have no talent for counting calories–and they have the figures to prove it.

He wrecked his car, lost his job, lost his house and yet throughout, he took his troubles like a man. He blamed them on his wife.

There are two sides to every story: the book and the movie.

He won't listen to his conscience. He doesn't want advice from a total stranger.

Have you noticed how close some people drive ahead of you?

The hardest commandments to live by are the first ten.

If you lend someone $100 and never see him again, it may be worth it.

Men consider a 20-mile hike keeping physically fit. Women call it shopping.

Criticism is one of the few things people would rather give than take.

When a man and woman marry, they become one...and then they discover which one.

The man who boasts he never made a mistake in his life may have a wife who did.

Always be tolerant of a person who disagrees with you. After all, he has a right to his ridiculous opinion.

To really enjoy your garden work, put on a wide hat and gloves, hold a trowel in one hand, and tell the man where to dig.

You are getting old if it takes you longer to rest than it did to get tired.

A conceited person has at least one good point: he doesn't talk about other people.

If you don't believe in luck, how else do you explain the success of those you don't like?

A fool and his money are soon invited to the best parties.

The only people who listen to both sides of an argument are the next-door neighbors.

The average time between throwing something out and needing it again is about two weeks.

There are bigger things in life than money: bills.

Money may still talk, but every year it makes less cents.

Don't worry if you start to lose your memory. Just forget about it.

The blonde at the next desk was using the following password: MickeyMinniePlutoDonaldDaisyHueyLouieDewey.

Why use such a long password? she was asked.

"Because it says it has to be 8 characters long."

Alcohol doesn't make you FAT. It makes you LEAN ... against table, chairs, floors, and ugly people.

Married men revealed that they perform the following act twice as often as single men:

Change their underwear.

Claustrophobia: fear of Santa Claus

Note from a teacher to parents on the first day of school: "If you promise not to believe everything your child says happens at school, I'll promise not to believe everything he says happens at home."

Age only matters if you're wine.

Consumption of alcohol may create the illusion that you are tougher, handsomer and smarter than some really really big guy named Tony.

What's the difference between a lawyer and a liar? The pronunciation.

A procrastinator's job is never done.

A husband was asked if he talked to his wife after sex. His answer: "Depends, if I'm near a phone."

Husbands are like fires. They go out if left unattended.

SLOGANS FOR WOMEN'S TSHIRTS

I'm out of estrogen, but I have a gun

Guys have feelings, too. But who cares?

I don't believe in miracles. I rely on them.

And your point is...

I'm busy. You're ugly. Have a nice day.

Warning! Next mood swing, 6 minutes

You have the right to remain silent, so please SHUT UP!

I'm one of those bad things that happen to good people.

Of course I don't look busy. I did it right the FIRST TIME

How can I miss you if you won't go away?

I read recipes the same way I read science fiction. I get to the end and think, "Well, that's not going to happen."

A woman needs a man like a fish needs a bicycle.

PREGNANCY Q AND A

Q: Should I have a baby after 35?
A: No, 35 children is quite enough.

Q: What's the most reliable method to determine the baby's sex?
A: Childbirth

Q: My childbirth instructor says I won't feel pain during labor, but pressure. Is she right?
A: Yes, in the same way a tornado might be called an air current.

Q: Is there anything I should avoid while recovering from childbirth?
A: Yes! Pregnancy.

Q: Do I have to have a baby shower?
A: Not if you change the baby's diaper very quickly.

Q: Our baby was born last week. When will my wife begin to feel and act normal again?
A: When the kids are in college.

Remember: if the world didn't suck, we'd all fall off.

What do you call a song sung in an automobile? A cartoon.

MORE WORDS OF WISDOM FROM STEVEN WRIGHT

Black holes are where God divided by zero.

If everything seems to be going well, you have obviously overlooked something.

Depression is merely anger without enthusiasm.

I couldn't repair your brakes so I made your horn louder.

Bills travel through the mail at twice the speed of checks.

The hardness of the butter is proportional to the softness of the bread.

Why do psychics have to ask for your name?

How do you know when you run out of invisible ink?

The colder the X-ray table, the more of your body is required on it.

I'd kill for a Nobel Peace Prize.

I intend to live forever. So far, so good.

When I'm not in my right mind, my left mind gets pretty crowded.

How many Californians does it take to change a lightbulb?
Six. One to turn the bulb, one for support, and four to relate to the experience.

How many psychiatrists does it take?
Only one, but the bulb must really want to change.

How many feminists does it take?
That's not funny!

How many software people does it take?
None. That's a hardware problem.

How many Calvinists does it take?
None. God has predestined when the light will come on.

How many Baptists?
CHANGE? But we never change!

How many Pentecostals?
Ten. One to change the bulb and nine to pray against the spirit of darkness.

How many TV evangelists?
One. But for the light to continue, send in your donation, thankyouverymuch!

How many Jewish mothers to change a lightbulb?
Never mind, I'll just sit here in the dark.

Since a lawyer joined our nudist colony, he hasn't had a suit.

Marriage is a three-ring circus: an engagement ring...a wedding ring...and suffering.

What do you call a lawyer with an IQ of 50? Senator.

Consumption of alcohol may lead you to think that people are laughing WITH you.

Health nuts are going to feel stupid someday, lying in hospitals dying of nothing.

Whenever I feel blue, I start breathing again.

Forget health food. I need all the preservatives I can get.

According to a recent survey, men say the first thing they notice about a woman is their eyes. And women say the first thing they notice about men is that they're a bunch of liars.

NAMES WE GIVE TO GROUPS OF ANIMALS

Pride of lions ...Murder of crows (also rooks and ravens) ... School of fish ... Exaltation of doves

Parliament of owls...Congress of baboons, the loudest, most dangerous and viciously aggressive of all primates.

MORE REALLY AWFUL COUNTRY WESTERN SONGS

I've Been Flushed from the Bathroom of Your Heart

I Changed Her Oil, She Changed My Life

If You Don't Leave Me Alone I'll Go and Find Someone Else Who Will

I Fell in a Pile of You and Got Love All Over Me

They May Put Me in Prison but They Can't Stop My Face from Breaking Out

My John Deere Was Breaking Your Field While Your Dear John Was Breaking My Heart

Thank God and Greyhound, She's Gone

I Keep Forgettin' I Forgot About You

She Got the Gold Mine and All I Got Was the Shaft

You're the Reason our Kids are So Ugly

Drop-Kick Me, Jesus, Through the Goal Posts of Life

How Can I Miss You if You Won't Go Away

I Got the Hungries for your Love and I'm Waitin' in Your Welfare Line

GREAT FEMALE COMEBACKS TO BAD PICKUP LINES

"I'd like to call you. What's your number?"
"It's in the phone book."
"But I don't know your name."
"That's in the phonebook, too."

"Haven't we met before?"
"Might be. I'm the receptionist at the VD clinic."

"Your place or mine?"
"Both. You go to yours and I'll go to mine."

"I'm here to fulfill your every sexual fantasy."
"You mean you have both a donkey and a Great Dane?"

"So, baby, what do you do for a living?"
"I'm a female impersonator."

"How do you like your eggs in the morning?"
"Unfertilized."

"I'd go to the end of the world for you."
"Yeah, but would you stay there?"

"If I throw a stick, will you leave?"

"Please! Off my planet!"

We all have to go sometime... so go now.

HOW TO DRIVE YOUR FELLOW WORKERS CRAZY

Page yourself over the intercom and don't disguise your voice.

Put your trash can on your desk and label it IN.

Put decaf in the coffee maker for 3 weeks. Once everyone has recovered from their caffeine addiction, switch to espresso.

Practice making fax and modem noises.

Reply to everything with "That's what you think."

Put mosquito netting around your cubicle.

Don't use any punctuation in your memos.

TYPE ONLY IN UPPERCASE.

type only in lowercase.

Answer your phone by saying, "The Morgue."

Pride, commitment, teamwork: words we use to get you to work for free.

You have the right to remain silent. Anything you say will be misquoted, then used against you.

Doctors can be frustrating. You wait six weeks for an appointment, and she says, "I wish you'd come to me sooner."

The other night I went to a real nice family restaurant. Every table had an argument going.

A fool and his money are a girl's best friend.

Madness takes its toll. Please have exact change.

Time is the best teacher. Unfortunately, it kills all its students.

It's not hard to meet expenses. They're everywhere.

Back up my hard drive? How do I put it in reverse?

Reality is the main obstacle to happiness.

The two most common elements in the universe and hydrogen and stupidity.

Death is life's way of telling you you've been fired.

All that glitters has a high refractive index.

If at first you do succeed, try not to look astonished.

Guns don't kill people; postal workers do.

Puritanism: the haunting fear that someone, somewhere, may be happy.

He who laughs last, thinks slowest.

He who hesitates is not only lost, but miles from the next exit.

I used up all my sick days. So I called in dead.

If you remember the '60s, you weren't really there.

Learn from your parents' mistakes. Use birth control.

Happiness is seeing your mother-in-law on a milk carton.

Give me ambiguity or give me something else.

Age only matters if you're cheese.

The imaginary friends I had as a kid dropped me because their friends thought I didn't exist.

He who laughs, lasts.

If all the cars in the United States were placed end to end, it would probably be the Fourth of July.

Television: a medium. So called because it is neither rare nor well-done. -Ernie Kovaks

The trouble with being on time is that there's nobody there to appreciate it.

I know that there are people in this world who do not love their fellow man, and I hate people like that! -Tom Lehrer

The metric system did not really catch on in the United States, unless you count the increasing popularity of the nine millimeter bullet. -Dave Barry

As a teenager, you are in the last stage of your life where you will be happy to hear that the phone call is for you.

Middle age is when you burn the midnight oil around 9:00 PM.

I'm sitting here thinking how nice it is that wrinkles don't hurt.

Not all men are annoying. Some are dead.

Earth is full. Go home.

Just give me chocolate and nobody gets hurt.

Age is a very high price to pay for maturity.

I base most of my fashion taste on what doesn't itch. -Gilda Radner

When women are depressed, they either eat or go shopping. Men invade another country.

Lincoln Kennedy, Oakland Raiders tackle, on his decision not to vote: "I was going to write myself in, but I was afraid I'd get shot."

Coach to a player who has received four F's and one D. "Son, it looks to me like you're spending too much time on one subject."

For three days after death, hair and fingernails continue to grow, but phone calls taper off.

Children in the back of the car cause accidents. Accidents in the back of the car cause children.

Don't give up. Moses was once a basket case.

A day without sunshine is like a day in Seattle.

God is love, but get it in writing.

Don't hate yourself in the morning. Sleep until noon.

I'm taking the scenic route through life.

No one has ever complained of a parachute not opening.

The first commandment was when Eve told Adam to take a bite of the apple.

Take my advice; I don't use it anyway.

If only you could get that wonderful feeling of accomplishment without having to do anything

If they can put one man on the moon, why can't they put them all there?

A fool and his money are soon elected.

A lawyer is someone who writes an 80-page document and calls it a brief.

Except for ending slavery, Fascism, the Nazi party, and Communism, war has never solved anything.

What do you call a man with no arms or legs, hanging on the wall? Art.

WHY DOGS ARE BETTER THAN WIVES

Dogs love it when your friends come over.

Dogs think you sing great.

The later you are, the more excited dogs are to see you.

Dogs never ask you if they look fat.

If a dog is gorgeous, other dogs don't hate it.

Dogs don't shop.

Dogs like it when you leave a mess on the floor.

Dogs will forgive you for playing with other dogs.

Dogs don't worry about germs.

Dogs don't expect gifts.

Dogs have no use for flowers, cards, or jewelry.

Dogs can't talk.

Dogs seldom outlive you.

Dogs don't mind if you give their offspring away.

THE WONDERFUL ERMA BOMBECK SPEAKS:

I take a very practical view of raising children. I put a sign in each of their rooms: "Checkout Time is 18 yrs."

I come from a family where gravy is considered a beverage.

If a man watches three football games in a row, he should be declared legally dead.

If you can't make it better, you can laugh at it.

Marriage has no guarantees. If that's what you're looking for, go live with a car battery.

In two decades, I've lost a total of 789 pounds. I should be hanging from a charm bracelet.

I've exercised with women so thin that buzzards followed them to their cars.

Did you ever notice that the first piece of luggage on the carousel never belongs to anyone?

Don't confuse fame with success. Madonna is one; Helen Keller is the other.

Guilt: the gift that keeps on giving.

Doctor, Doctor, I tend to flush a lot.
Don't worry, it's just a chain reaction.

Doctor, doctor, I keep thinking I'm a bee.
Buzz off, can't you see I'm busy?

Doctor, doctor, everyone keeps throwing me in the garbage.
Don't talk rubbish!

Doctor, doctor, I feel like a sheep.
That's baaaaaaad!

Doctor, doctor, I feel like a pack of cards.
I'll deal with you later.

Doctor, doctor, I keep thinking there is two of me.
One at a time, please.

Doctor, doctor, will this ointment clear up my spots?
I never make rash promises

Doctor, doctor, I suffer from deja vu.
Didn't I see you yesterday?

The most precious thing we have is life. Yet it has absolutely no trade-in value.

Too much of a good thing can be wonderful.

SPORTS QUOTES

"We can't win at home. We can't win on the road. As general manager, I just can't figure out where else to play." –Orlando Magic general manager, 1992

"He's a guy who gets up at six o'clock in the morning regardless of what time it is." -veteran boxing trainer

"One player was lost because he broke his nose. How do you go about getting a nose into condition for football?" -Texas football coach, 1966

"The team's co-captain pulled a hamstring running onto the field for the coin toss. I'm going to send the injured reserve players out for the toss next time." -Baltimore Colts coach, 1981

"I'm not allowed to comment on lousy officiating." -general manager, New Orleans Saints, 1986

Dorothy Shula, on the career dedication of her husband, the Miami Dolphins' coach: "I'm fairly confident that if I died tomorrow, Don would find a way to preserve me until the season was over and he had time for a nice funeral."

Hugh Campbell, football coach at Whitworth College, after his team defeated Whitman 70-30: "It wasn't as easy as you think. It's hard to stay awake that long."

The first rule of holes: if you are in one, stop digging.

I wish the buck stopped here. I could use a few.

I went to school to become a wit... only got halfway through.

It was all so different before everything changed.

I recently became a Christian Scientist. It was the only health plan I could afford.

Love thy enemy. That'll confuse the hell out of them.

Men wake up looking as good as they did when they went to sleep.
Women somehow deteriorate during the night.

Women and cats will do exactly as they please, and men and dogs should relax and get used to it.

Her husband came home with a tube of KY jelly and said, "This will make you happy tonight." He was right. When he left the bedroom, she squirted it all over the doorknob. He couldn't get back in.

Inside every old person is a young person, wondering, "What the hell happened?"

We'll be old friends until we're old and senile. Then we'll be new friends.

Why is "overlook" so different from "oversee?"

Soldier: If we do happen to step on a mine, sir, what do we do?

Captain: Normal procedure is to jump 200 feet in the air and scatter oneself over a wide area.

Sometimes I lie awake at night and I ask, "Where have I gone wrong?" Then a voice says to me, "This is going to take more than one night."

Time's fun when you're having flies.

–Kermit the frog

How do you get off a non-stop flight?

A vasectomy means never having to say you're sorry.

A psychiatrist is a man who asks you a lot of expensive questions your wife asks for free.

He was happily married. But his wife wasn't.

Do infants have as much fun in infancy as adults have in adultery?

WHY MEN ARE HAPPIER THAN WOMEN

Men can play with toys all their life.

Men can wear shorts no matter what their legs look like.

Men don't have to stop and think which way to turn the screw.

Men can go on a week's vacation and pack one small case.

Men can keep the same hairstyle for years, even decades.

The whole garage belongs to them.

Men can decide whether or not to grow a mustache.

Men have one wallet and one pair of shoes which are good for every season and every need.

Weddings take care of themselves.

Men's new shoes never cut, blister or mangle their feet.

Men can open all their own jars.

Men's wrinkles add character.

WHY DID THE CHICKEN CROSS THE ROAD?

NY Police Department: Give us five minutes with the chicken. He'll tell us what we need to know.

Karl Marx: It was an historical inevitability.

Aristotle: It is in the nature of chickens to cross roads.

Dr. Seuss: Did the chicken cross the road? Did he cross it with a toad? Yes! The chicken crossed the road, but why it crossed, I've not been told!

Capt. James T. Kirk: To boldly go where no chicken has gone before.

Ernest Hemingway: To die. In the rain.

Bill Gates: Just released: Chicken 1.2 which will not only cross the road, but will lay eggs on it.

George W. Bush: What chicken was that?

Colonel Sanders: I missed one?

Grandpa: In my day, we didn't ask why the chicken crossed the road. We were told that the chicken crossed the road and that was good enough for us.

Don't you wish there was a setting on the TV that would turn up the intelligence? There's one marked "brightness" but I can't get it to work.

Don't let your mind wander. It's too little to be let out alone.

36 years old is significant; because, at 36, you can sleep with someone half your age and not be put in jail.

NOTICE: Princess, having had sufficient experiences with Princes, seeks frog.

My grandmother is 90 and still doesn't need glasses. Drinks right out of the bottle.
-Henny Youngman

Responsible drinking? Now, that's an oxymoron.

Life is like a taxi... it just keeps right on ticking, whether you're getting anywhere or not.

Nothing is as frustrating as arguing with someone who knows what she's talking about.

I think I've discovered the secret of life ... you just hang around until you get used to it.
-Chas. Shultz

Learn to be sincere, even if you have to fake it.

Never do anything you wouldn't want to have to explain to the paramedics.

Never put off until tomorrow what you can avoid completely.

An optimist is someone who falls off the Empire State Building and, as he passes the 50th floor, thinks, "So far, so good."

Minds are like parachutes. They only work when they are open.

Love your enemies. At least they never try to borrow money from you.

If electricity hadn't been invented, we'd all be watching television by candlelight. -Geo. Gobel

I try to avoid cliches like the plague.

The government is like a baby's alimentary canal, with a happy appetite at one end and no responsibility at the other. -Pres. R. Reagan

The inherent vice of capitalism is the unequal sharing of the blessings. The inherant blessing of socialism is the equal sharing of misery.
-Winston Churchill

A man is incomplete until he marries. Then he's finished.

ABOUT GETTING OLDER

Eventually, you will reach a point when you stop lying about your age and start bragging about it.

The older we get, the fewer things seem worth waiting in line for.

Some people try to turn back their odometers. Not me. I want people to know why I look this way. I've traveled a long way and some of the roads weren't paved.

My grandmother's dating. She's 90, he's 93. It's going great. They never argue. They can't hear each other.

You know you are getting old when everything either dries up or leaks.

I don't know how I got over the hill without getting to the top.

One of the many things no one tells you about aging is that it's such a nice change from being young.

Being young is beautiful, but being old is comfortable.

One must wait until evening to see how splendid the day has been.

MENTAL HOSPITAL PHONE MENU
Please select from the following options:

*If you are obsessive-compulsive, press 1 repeatedly.

*If you are co-dependent, please ask someone to press 2 for you.

*If you have multiple personalities, press 3, 4, and 5.

*If you are paranoid, we know who you are and what you want. Stay on the line so we can trace your call.

*If you are delusional, press 7 and your call will be forwarded to the Mother Ship.

*If you are schizophrenic, listen carefully and a voice will tell you which number to press.

*If you are bipolar, leave a message after the beep or before the beep or after the beep. Wait for the beep.

*If you are dyslexic, press 969696969696969696.

*If you have short-term memory loss, press 8. If you have short-term memory loss, press 8. If you have short-term memory loss, press 8.

*If you suffer from low self-esteem, please hang up. Our operators are too busy to help you.

WASHINGTON POST POETRY COMPETITION: THE MOST ROMANTIC FIRST LINE AND THE LEAST ROMANTIC SECOND LINE

I want to feel your sweet embrace;
But keep the paper bag upon your face.

I thought that I could love no other–
that is, until I met your brother.

I love your smile, your face, your eyes–
Damn, I'm good at telling lies!

My love, you take my breath away.
What've you stepped in to smell this way?

My feelings for you no words can tell,
Except for maybe, "Go to Hell."

I see your face when I am dreaming.
That's why I always wake up screaming.

Kind, intelligent, loving and hot;
This describes everything you are not.

My darling, my lover, my beautiful wie,
Marrying you sure screwed up my life.

What inspired this amorous rhyme?
Two parts tequila, one part lime.

Give a person a fish and you feed them for a day. Teach a person to use the internet and they won't bother you for weeks.

Men have two emotions: hungry and horny. If you see him without an erection, make him a sandwich.

Banging your head against a wall uses 150 calories an hour. Hardly seems worth it.

If time and space are curved, where do all the straight people come from?

My children refused to eat anything that hadn't danced on TV. -Erma Bombeck

It is better to trip and end up on the floor than not to trip and end up on the floor for no particular reason.

The day after tomorrow is the third best day of your life.

If we were meant to fly, we wouldn't keep losing our luggage.

Anything not nailed down is a cat toy.

There's a thin person inside every fat person. I ate mine.

THE THINGS KIDS SAY

THE THINGS KIDS SAY

A father watched his young daughter playing in the garden. How sweet and innocent she looked, smelling the flowers and examining the moss between the rock walkway. Suddenly she stopped and stared at the ground. Curious, he went to see what work of nature had captured her attention. It was two spiders mating.

"Daddy, what are they doing?" she asked.

"They're mating."

"Who is the spider on top?"

"Daddy Longlegs," said the father.

"So the other one is a Mommy longlegs?"

"No, darling, both of them are Daddy Longlegs."

The little girl stared for a moment, then stomped the spiders flat, saying, "Well, we're not having any of that Brokeback Mountain shit in *our* garden!"

Beethoven wrote music, even though he was deaf. He was so deaf, he wrote very loud music.

–7-year-old Henry

KIDS WRITE ABOUT THE BIBLE

In the first book of the Bible, Guinesses, God got tired of creating the world so he took the Sabbath off.

The Jews were a proud people and throughout history they had trouble with unsympathetic genitals.

Moses led the Jews to the Red Sea where they made unleavened bread, which is bread without any ingredients.

Noah built an ark and the animals came on in pears.

Adam and Eve were created from an apple tree.

Noah's wife was Joan of Ark.

Solomon, one of David's sons, had 300 wives and 700 porcupines.

Joshua led the Hebrews in the Battle of Geritol.

Moses went up to Mount Cyanide.

God said, "Give me a light," and someone did.

David was a Hebrew king who was skilled at playing the lair. He fought the Finkelsteins, a race of people who lived in Biblical times.

When Mary heard she was the mother of Jesus, she sang the Magna Carta.

St. Paul cavorted to Christianity. He preached holy acrimony, which is another name for marriage.

When the three wise guys from the East Side arrived, they found Jesus in the manager.

Moses died before he ever reached Canada.

Lot's wife was a pillar of salt during the day but a ball of fire at night.

Sampson was a strongman who let himself be led astray by a Jezebel like Delilah.

The greatest miracle in the Bible is when Joshua told his son to stand still, and he obeyed.

It was a miracle when Jesus rose from the dead and managed to move the tombstone off the entrance.

Christians have only one spouse. This is called monotony.

The Bible says the Lord thy God is one; but I think he must be older than that.

Adam and Eve had a son, Cain, who hated his brother as long as he was Abel.

Adam and Eve disobeyed God by eating one bad apple, so they were driven from the Garden of Eden. Not sure what they were driven in though, because they didn't have cars.

Adam and Eve were naked, but they weren't embarrassed because mirrors hadn't been invented yet.

After the Old Testament came the New Testament. Jesus is the star of The New. He was born in Bethlehem in a barn. (I wish I had been born in a barn too, because my mom is always saying to me, "Close the door! Were you born in a barn?" It would be nice to say, "As a matter of fact, I was.")

During his life, Jesus had many arguments with sinners like the Pharisees and the Democrats.

The worst one was Judas Asparagus. He was so evil they named a terrible vegetable after him.

The first grade teacher asked if anyone in her class knew what an ambassador is. A little girl's hand shot up. "Yes, that's what my Mom calls my Dad when they're fighting."

My young grandson called the other day to wish me a happy birthday. He asked how old I was, and I told him 62.

He was quiet for a long moment, and then he asked: "Did you start at one?"

She was in the bathroom putting on her makeup under the watchful eyes of young granddaughter as she'd done many times before. After she applied her lipstick and started to leave, the child said, "Gramma, you forgot to kiss the toilet paper goodbye."

When my grandson Billy and I entered our vacation cabin, we kept the lights off until we were inside to keep from attracting pesky insects. Still, a few fireflies followed us in. Noticing them, Billy whispered: "It's no good, Grandpa. Now the mosquitoes are coming after us with flashlights."

An honest 7-year-old told her parents that Billy Brown had kissed her after class. "How did that happen?" asked her surprised mother. "It wasn't easy," admitted the girl. "But three girls helped me catch him."

The Kindergarten teacher said, "If you have to go to the bathroom, hold up two fingers." Said a little boy in the back: "How will that help?"

A little girl, new to American history, wrote: "Abraham Lincoln's mother died in infancy. He was born in a log cabin he built with his own hands."

Q: Briefly explain what hard water is.
A: Ice

Q: Name one of the early Romans' greatest achievements.
A: Leaning to speak Latin

Q: Name the wife of Orpheus, whom he attempted to save from the Underworld.
A: Mrs. Orpheus

Q: Name six animals which live in the Arctic.
A: Two polar bears and four seals.

Q: Where was the American Declaration of Independence signed?
A: At the bottom

Q: What is the meaning of "varicose?"
A: Close by

Q: Where was Hadrian's Wall built?
A: Around Hadrian's garden.

TEACHER: Donald, what is the chemical formula for water?

DONALD: H I J K L M N O

TEACHER: What are you talking about?

DONALD: Yesterday you said it was H to O.

TEACHER: Virginia, name one important thing we have today we didn't have ten years ago.

VIRGINIA: Me!

TEACHER: Jake, why are you doing your multiplication work on the floor?

JAKE: You said to do it without using tables.

TEACHER: Ellen, go to the map and find North America.

ELLEN: It's right here.

TEACHER: Correct. Now class, who discovered America?

CLASS: Ellen!

H2O is hot water, and CO2 is cold water.

The pistol of a flower is its only protection against insects.

Q: What happens to a boy when he enters puberty?

A: He says goodbye to his childhood and hello to his adultery.

KIDS FINISH FAMILIAR PROVERBS

Strike while the . . . bug is close.

A bird in the hand . . . is going to poop on you.

Children should be seen and not . . . spanked or grounded.

A miss is as good as a . . . Mrs.

If at first you don't succeed . . . get new batteries.

Don't bite the hand that . . . looks dirty.

No news is . . . impossible.

When the blind lead the blind . . . get out of the way.

Two's company, three's . . .the Musketeers.

An idle mind is . . . the best way to relax.

There are none so blind as . . .Stevie Wonder.

Better late than . . . pregnant.

Love all, trust . . . me.

Writing at the same time as Shakespeare was Miguel Cervantes. He wrote Donkey Hote. The next great author was John Milton. Milton wrote Paradise Lost. Then his wife died and he wrote Paradise Regained. –6th grade student

Little Johnny watched, fascinated, as his mother smoothed cold cream on her face.

"Why do you do that, Mommy?" he asked.

"To make myself beautiful," said his mother, who then began removing the cream with a tissue.

"What's the matter?" asked Little Johnny. "Giving up?"

A new teacher was trying to make use of her psychology courses. She started her class by saying, "Everyone who thinks they're stupid, please stand up." After a few minute, one little boy stood. "Do you think you're stupid?" asked the teacher.

"No, ma'am, but I hate to see you standing up there all by yourself."

TEACHER: Marie, give me a sentence starting with "I."

MARIE: I is...

TEACHER: No, no, Marie... Always say "I am."

MARIE: All right. I am the ninth letter of the alphabet.

Equator: a menagerie lion running around the earth through Africa.

KIDS ON LOVE AND MARRIAGE

You got to find somebody who likes the same stuff. Like, if you like sports, she should like it that you like sports, and she should keep the chips and dip coming. –Alan, age 10

No person really decides before they grow up who they're going to marry. God decides it all way before, and you get to find out later who you're stuck with. -Camille, age 10

Twenty-three is the best age to get married because you know the person FOREVER by then.
-Lori, age 10

You have to guess whether two people are married, based on whether they seem to be yelling at the same kids. -Derek, age 8

What do my Mom and Dad have in common? They both don't want any more kids. -Laura, age 8

Dates are for having fun, and people could use them to get to know each other. Even boys have something to say if you listen long enough.
-Lynn, age 8

It's okay to kiss someone when they're rich.
-Pam, age 7

It's better for girls to be single but not for boys. Boys need someone to clean up after them.
-Anita, age 9

To make a marriage work, you should tell your wife she looks pretty, even if she looks like a dump truck. -Rick, age 10

If people didn't get married, there sure would be a lot of kids to explain, wouldn't there?
-Alex, age 8

The law says you have to be eighteen to kiss someone so I wouldn't want to mess with that.
-Tyler, age 7

The rule about kissing goes like this: if you kiss someone, then you should marry them and have kids with them. It's the right thing to do.
-Henry, age 8

A little boy and a little girl were at day care one day. The girl said to the boy, "Tommy, want to play house?"

"Okay," he says. "What should I do?"

"Communicate your feelings."

"Communicate my feelings? I don't know what that means."

"Perfect," says the little girl. "You can be the husband."

When God made the world, he split the Adam and made Eve. -Asher, age 7

Ms. Evans taught science in a Tennessee school. She was trying to teach evolution and the class was arguing with her. Bobby raised his hand and said, "But I thought God created the world and everything in it."

Said the teacher: "Can you see God?"

"No," he replied.

"Hear God?"

"No."

"Feel God?"

"No."

"Well, then, how do we know that God exists?"

Bobby leaned over and whispered to his friend Joey, "Can you see Ms Evan's brain? No. So it must not exist."

Five-year-old Becky came to the door when the census taker came by. She told the guy that her Daddy wasn't home because he was at work performing an appendectomy.

"My," said the census taker, "That's a very big word for such a little girl. Do you know what it means?"

"Sure do! Fifteen-hundred bucks and that doesn't include the anesthesiologist!"

4-year-old: "What if Jesus had been a girl?"

TEACHER: Zeke, why are you always so dirty?
STUDENT: Well, I'm a lot closer to the ground than you are.

TEACHER: Now, Will, tell me, do you say prayers before eating?
STUDENT: No, I don't have to. My Mom is a good cook.

TEACHER: Parker, what do you call a person who keeps on talking when people are no longer interested?
STUDENT: A teacher!

A very dirty little boy came in from playing in the yard and asked his mother, "Who am I?"

Ready to play the game, she said, "I don't know. Who are you?"

"Wow!" cried the child. "Mrs. Adams was right! She said I was so dirty, my own mother wouldn't recognize me!"

A man and his wife hosted a dinner party for people from his job, including his boss. All during dinner, the host's 3-year-old girl stared at her father's boss, stared so hard at him that he became uncomfortable. Finally, he asked her, "Why are you staring at me?" Everyone at the table waited for her answer. She said, "My Daddy said you drink like a fish and I don't want to miss it!"

TEACHER: Why are you late?
STUDENT: Class started before I got here.

Little Bobby asked his mother for a nickel. "What did you do with the money I gave you yesterday?" she asked. "I gave it to a poor old lady," he said. "What a good boy! Here is another nickel. But how did you become so interested in this poor old lady?"

"She's the one who sells the candy."

The Kindergarten teacher was reading The Three Little Pigs to her class.

"And the pig went up to the man who was selling straw, and he said, 'Please, sir, may I buy some of that straw to build my house?'

"And what do you think the man said?" asked the teacher.

A little boy raised his hand and said, "I know! I know! 'Holy smoke, a talking pig!'"

The teacher was unable to continue for the next five minutes.

In an earth science class, the teacher was lecturing on map reading. After explaining latitude, longitude, degrees and minutes, she asked, "Suppose I asked you to meet me for lunch at 23 degrees, 4 minutes North latitude and 45 degrees, 15 minutes East longitude?"

After a confused silence, a voice volunteered, "I guess you'd be eating alone."

This a riddle answered correctly by 80% of a Kindergarten, compared to 17% of University seniors.

What is greater than God?
More evil than Satan?
The poor have it.
The rich need it.
And if you eat it, you'll die.
What is it?

The answer: NOTHING

Finding one of her students making ugly faces at his classmates during recess, Ms. Smith gently reproved the child.

Smiling sweetly, she said, "When I was your age, I was told that if I made ugly faces, they would freeze and I would have them forever."

The child answered, "Well, Ms. Smith, you can't say you weren't warned."

During a lesson in world religions, a Kindergarten teacher asked her students to bring to class something related to their family's faith.

The first child called up to the front of the room said: "I am Muslim and this is my prayer rug."

The second child said, "I am Jewish and this is my Star of David."

The third child said, "I am Catholic and this is my rosary."

The fourth child said, "I am Southern Baptist and this is my casserole dish."

Little Tommy was doing very badly in math. Nothing seemed to help, not tutors, nor flash cards, not even a special Learning Center. Finally, they enrolled him in a Catholic School which turned out very well-educated students.

The first day, Tommy came home, looking very serious, and went straight upstairs to do his homework. After supper, instead of playing video games, he went back to work. And that is how it went, week after week. Tommy did his homework diligently. His mother was happy, but concerned.

When he came home with an A in math, she could no longer stay silent. "Tommy, I am very pleased with your progress. But what made you decide to work so hard? The nuns? The rules? The discipline? What? Please tell me."

Said Tommy, "Well, on the first day of school, when I saw that guy nailed to the plus sign, I knew they weren't kidding around."

Salesman at the door says: "Can I speak to your father?"

Little boy whispers, "He's busy, talking to the firefighters."

"Okay, then, can I speak with your mother?"

"She's busy, too."

"What's she doing?"

"Talking to the policeman."

"Let me get this straight. All the adults are busy with firefighters and police. What's going on?"

Whispers the boy: "They're looking for me!"

KID SCIENCE

*When you smell an odorless gas, it's probably carbon monoxide.

*The moon is a planet just like the earth, only it is even deader.

*Vacuum: a large empty space where the pope lives.

*Planet: a body of earth surrounded by sky.

*Rhubarb: a kind of celery gone bloodshot.

*Blood flows down one leg and up the other.

*Mushrooms grow in damp places, that's why they look like umbrellas.

*Respiration is composed of two acts: first, inspiration, and then expectoration.

*A super-saturated solution is one that holds more than it can hold.

*Before giving a blood transfusion, find out if the blood is affirmative or negative.

*Dew is formed on leaves when the sun shines on them and makes them perspire.

*The body consists of three parts – the branium, the borax, and the abdominable cavity. The brainium contains the brain. The borax contains the heart and lungs, and the abdominable cavity contains the bowels, of which there are five: a,e,i,o, and u.

MORE NEW ENDINGS TO PROVERBS:

When the blind lead the blind . . .get out of the way.

If you lie down with dogs, you'll . . . . stink in the morning.

If at first you don't succeed . . . . get new batteries.

Don't put off til tomorrow what . . . . you put on to go to bed.

Happy the bride who . . . . gets all the presents.

A penny saved is . . . . not much money.

It's always darkest before . . . . Daylight Savings Time.

Better to be safe than . . . . punch a fifth-grader.

You can't teach an old dog new . . . . math.

Laugh and the world laughs with you, cry and you ... have to blow your nose.

A little boy asked his grandmother how old she was.

"Thirty-nine and holding," she told him.

"Well, how old would you be if you let go?"

A little girl was watching her parents dress for a formal party. When she saw that her father was putting on his tuxedo, she said, "Daddy, you shouldn't wear that suit."

"Why not?" he asked.

"Because it always gives you a headache the next day."

When I worked for Meals on Wheels, delivering food to the home-bound elderly, I would take my four-year-old daughter with me. She was always fascinated with the appliances of old age: the canes and the walkers and the wheelchairs.

One day, I saw her staring at a set of false teeth in a glass of cleaner.

She looked up and said, "The tooth fairy will never believe this!"

At the end of the working day, a policeman parked his van in front of the station and his dog started barking. After stowing his gear, he noticed a puzzled-looking little boy standing nearby. "Is that a dog you have back there?" the boy asked.

"Yes, it is," said the policeman.

"What did he do?"

One warm summer evening, a mother was driving with her three young children. A woman in the convertible in front of them suddenly stood up and waved. She was stark naked. As the mother was reeling from the shock, wondering what she was going to say to her kids, the five year old said, "Mom, that lady isn't wearing a seat belt!"

A mother was ironing some clean shirts one day. Her little boy asked, "Mommy, why are you ironing the shirts?"

She said, "To take out all the wrinkles and make them nice and smooth."

"Then why don't you iron Grandma's face?"

A young boy was having a bit of a temper tantrum and when his mother told him to go to his room to calm down, he said, "That's dumb! And you're dumb!" She then said he would stay twice as long in his room for saying such a terrible thing to her; and she wanted him to think about what he had said while he was alone in his room.

After around fifteen minutes, she went to his room to see if he was repentant. He had calmed down and stopping crying. "I see that you have done some thinking here in your room," she said.

"Yes," he answered. "But, Mom, you really are dumb."

"Children, why are we quiet in church?"

"Because people are sleeping!"

"Oh, boy! I'm glad you're here," the little boy said to his grandmother.

"Why?" she asked.

"Because now Daddy will do the trick he's been promising us."

"What trick is that?"

"He told Mommy that if you come to visit, he would climb the walls."

Eric was asked by his mother what he had learned in Sunday School.

"Well, Mommy, our teacher told us how God sent Moses behind enemy lines on a rescue mission to lead the Israelites out of Egypt. And when he got to the Red Sea, he had his engineers build a pontoon bridge and all the people walked across. Then he used his walkie-talkie to radio HQ for reinforcements and they sent bombers to blow up the bridge so that all the Egyptian soldiers were drowned."

"Now, Eric, is that really what your teacher taught you?"

"Well, no, Mom, but if I told it the way the teacher did, you'd never believe it."

Seeing his father tapping on a wall to find the studs, so he could hang some pictures, a six-year-old said, "Daddy, there's no one in there."

Told to behave, the two-year-old said to his mother, "I'm being haive!"

A young mother was walking with her small daughter one day when the little girl picked something up off the ground and started to put in into her mouth. The mother stopped her and said she should never do that."

"Why?" asked the little girl.

"Because it's dirty. It's been on the ground. People have probably stepped on it with their dirty shoes and it's got lots of germs."

The child looked at her mother with admiration. "Mommy, how do you know so many things?"

Thinking quickly, the woman said, "All Mommys know a lot. We have to. It's on the Mommy Test. If you can't pass that test, you can't be a Mommy."

The little girl pondered that for a few minutes. Then, her face brightening, she said, "Oh, I get it! If you don't pass the test, you get to be a Daddy!"

"You got that right," said her mother.

The 3-year-old girl in the drugstore was trying to pick out a toy. "You must get a small toy," her mother told her, "Those are too expensive."

"Why don't you get some expensive money?" demanded the tot

A little girl in church for the first time, when the collection plate comes around, whispers loudly: "Don't pay for me, Daddy. I'm under five."

A man, watching his pre-teen daughter doing the dishes with somewhat less than full enthusiasm, suggested that she use some elbow grease.

"Really?" she replied. "Mom said all I had to use was the sponge and dish detergent."

In a preschool class I used to teach, there were two little girls who played every day that they were characters from classic Disney cartoons. One day, I heard one call the other one "Allison." I couldn't think of a single Disney character by that name; so I asked her who she was today.

"Allison Wonderland," was the reply.

The Sunday School teacher explained to her class that a hypocrite was someone who says one thing but feels quite differently. A girl, seven years old, asked, "Well, sometimes I say something really mean to my brother, but I feel really good inside. Does that mean I'm a hypocrite?"

A mother informed her little boy that his shoes were on the wrong feet. "Oh, no, Mommy," he said. "I'm sure they're my feet."

Overhead at the pediatrician's office, a boy to his mother: "You told me it would be a shot, but it was a needle!"

A child scolded for peeking at his Christmas presents: "I didn't see much! I have little eyes!"

A little boy was asked why he was digging through the box of animal crackers. "The box says you can't eat them if the seal is broken. I'm looking for the seal."

There were four newborn kittens and the 3-year-old in the household told his mother that there were two girl and two boy kittens. "How do you know that?" she asked. His reply: "Daddy picked them up and looked underneath. I think it's printed on the bottom."

Little girl is told to make up her mind. She asks, "How do you put makeup on your mind?"

Three-year-old to his bald but bearded father: "Daddy, did your hair slip?"

A grandmother was telling her little granddaughter what her own childhood had been like. "We used to ice skate outside on a pond. I had a swing made from a tire and it hung from a tree in the back yard. We rode on our pony. We picked raspberries in the woods in the back and then ate them with sugar and cream."

The little girl was wide-eyed, taking this in. Then, she said, "I sure wish I'd gotten to know you sooner."

A 7-year-old, overheard saying to his younger brother: "Tell me when you fall asleep, okay?"

The discussion in a class of 5- and 6-year-olds in Sunday School was about the Ten Commandments. After explaining what it meant to honor thy Father and thy Mother, the teacher asked, "Is there a commandment that teaches us how to treat our brothers and sisters?"

Without missing a beat, one little boy called out, "Thou shalt not kill!"

Overheard: a four-year-old girl, reciting the Lord's Prayer: "And lead us not into temptation, but deliver us some email..."

My grandson was visiting one day when he asked, "Nana, do you know how you and God are alike?" Mentally polishing my halo, I said, "No, honey, how are we alike?"

"You're both old."

A father was reading Bible stories to his young son. He read, "The man named Lot was warned to take his wife and flee out of the city without looking back; but his wife looked back and was turned to salt."

His son asked, "What happened to the flea?"

I called home one day and my 6-year-old answered the phone, panting a little.

"Hi, Nicky, you sound out of breath."

He replied: "No, Mommy, I have more."

WHAT IS A GRANDPARENT? KIDS ANSWER:

.Grandparents are a lady and a man who have no little children of their own. They like other peoples'.

.A grandfather is a man and a grandmother is a lady.

.They don't say "Hurry up."

.When they take us for walks, they slow down past things like pretty leaves and caterpillars.

.They wear glasses and funny underwear.

.When they read to us, they don't skip. They don't mind it if we ask for the same story over again.

.They have to answer questions like "why isn't God married?" and "how come dogs chase cats?"

.Everybody should try to have a grandmother and grandfather, especially if you don't have television, because they are the only grownups who like to spend time with us.

.Grandpa is the smartest man on earth. He teaches me good things but I don't get to see him enough to get as smart as him!

.Grandparents don't have to be smart.

My friend asked her grandson when he would be turning six. "When I'm tired of being five," he answered.

A little girl asked her mother, "Can I go outside and play with the boys?" Her mother said, "I don't think you should. They're too rough." After thinking about this for a few minutes, the girl said, "If I find a smooth one, can I play with him?"

Somebody's little boy asked if a cemetery is where dead people live.

Seeing her first hail, Julia, age 3, exclaimed, "Mommy, it's raining dumplings!"

Announcing to my granddaughter that her aunt had just had a baby and he looked just like his father, she said, "You mean he has a mustache?"

A little boy at the beach saw a dead seagull in the sand. He pulled his father to see it and said, "Daddy, what happened to him?"

"He died and went to heaven."

The boy thought this over and then said, "Why did God throw him back down?"

I can recall when my baby sister implored my Dad not to turn out the light in her room because she couldn't see how to sleep in the dark.

A mother was preparing pancakes for her two sons, Dave and Jay. The boys began to argue about who would get the first pancake off the griddle. Seeing an opportunity for a moral lesson, the mother said, "If Jesus were here, he'd say 'Give the first pancake to my brother. I can wait.'"

Dave turned to his younger brother. "Jay... you be Jesus."

Four-year-old Talia, on a drive through the Kentucky countryside, marveled at all the horse farms they passed. "Look, Mommy," she cried, as the car rounded the bend to yet another scenic green lawn, surrounded by white fencing, "there are some more of those horse-holding-in things!"

One child says: If you want a kitten, start out asking for a horse.

Another says: If you get a bad grade in school, show it to your Mom when she's on the phone.

A little girl advises: Don't use markers as lipstick.

Also: You can't hide a piece of broccoli in a glass of milk.

Also: When your Mom is mad at your Dad, don't let her brush your hair.

When little Josh overheard his parents saying that his beloved grandmother was a "pushover," he knew they were talking about the fact that she brought him many presents, let him do pretty much whatever he wanted, and thought he was a terrific little boy. So when she stayed overnight at his house, he woke his mother at 6 AM, saying, "Come on, let's push over Grandma."

Three boys are in the schoolyard, bragging about their fathers.

Boy One says, "My father scribbles some words on a piece of paper–he calls it a poem–and they give him $50."

Boy Two says, "My father scribbles some words on a piece of paper–he calls it a song– and they give him $100."

Boy Three says, "That's nothing. My Dad scribbles a few words on a piece of paper–he calls it a sermon–and it takes eight people to collect all the money!"

A Sunday School teacher asked her class why Joseph and Mary took Jesus with them to Jerusalem. A small child replied: "They couldn't get a babysitter."

A little boy was overheard praying: "Lord, if you can't make me a better boy, don't worry about it. I'm pretty happy the way that I am."

Three-year-old Tony: "Our father who does art in heaven, Harold is his name."

Two little boys, cousins, were attending their first family wedding. After the service, they discussed marriage. How many women could a man marry? The younger boy said, "I know. Sixteen." His older cousin was amazed that he knew the answer so confidently. "How do you know that?"

"Easy," said the younger one. "All you have to do is add it up. Four better, four worse, four richer, four poorer. Sixteen!"

A little girl, let's call her Emily, was dressed in her Sunday best and running as fast as she could, trying not to be late for Sunday School. As she ran, she prayed, "Dear Lord, please don't let me be late for Sunday School, please don't let me be late!"

While running and praying, she tripped on a curb and fell, tearing her dress and getting her knee socks dirty.

She got up, brushed herself off, and started to run again, praying, "Dear Lord, please don't let me be late ... but please, don't shove me, either!"

Two boys were walking home together from Bible School. One said to the other, "What do you think about all this Satan stuff?"

The other boy replied: "Well, you know how Santa Claus turned out. It's probably just our Dads."

At a Sunday School class, a teacher asked, "What was the name of Jesus' mother?"

A girl answered: "Mary."

The teacher then asked, "And who knows the name of Jesus' father?"

The same girl said, "Verge."

Confused, the teacher asked, "Where did you get that?"

Said the girl: "Well, they're always talking about Verge 'n' Mary."

Three-year-old Katie was found in her room, standing on her brother's toy cars. When reprimanded, she said: "But I'm only trying to make roller skates!"

Mary Ellen, 3 years old, came out of the bathroom, bearing an empty toilet paper roll. Her puzzled mother asked her how much paper she had used. Her answer: "Much and much."

Overheard by Zach's mother: "I'm fee. My sister is one. But I'm fee. I win!"

The two-year-old bumped her foot, and complained to her mother. "Mommy, I hurt my toe!" When Mommy didn't respond quickly, she added: "It's my all-the-way-home toe!"

One small boy to another: Why is it called the poop deck?

Attending a wedding for the first time, a little girl asked her mother why the bride was dressed in white. "Because white is the color of happiness," said her mother, "and this is the happiest day of her life."

"Then why," asked the child, "is the groom wearing black?"

Not quite getting it, the first grader said, "I led the pigeons to the flag."

How did God make Mothers?

.Magic plus super powers and a lot of stirring.

.He made my Mom the same way he made me, just with bigger parts.

.He used dirt, just like He used for the rest of us.

Why did God make Mothers?

.Think about it. It was the best way to get more people.

.To help us come out when we were getting born.

.Mainly to clean the house.

.She's the only one who knows where to find the scotch tape.

How did your Mother meet your Dad?

.Mommy was working in a store and Daddy was shoplifting.

Why did your mother marry your father?

.She got too old to do anything else with him.

.My grandma says that Mommy didn't have her thinking cap on.

.My Dad makes the best spaghetti in the world; and my Mom eats a lot.

Who's the boss around your house?

.My Mom doesn't want to be the boss but she has to because my Dad's such a goofball.

.Mom. You can tell by how she does room inspection. She sees the stuff under the bed.

.I guess my Mom is, but only because she has a lot more to do than my Dad.

What's the difference between Dads and Moms?

.Dads are stronger and taller, but Moms have the real power cause that's who you gotta ask if you want to sleep over at your friend's.

.Moms know how to talk to teachers without scaring them.

.Moms work at work and work at home while Dads only work at work.

What does your mother do in her spare time?

.Mothers don't do spare time.

.To hear her tell it, she pays bills all day long.

.She just cleans and cleans and cooks and cooks.

KIDS'-EYE VIEW OF SCIENCE

When scientists broke open molecules, they found they were only stuffed with atoms. But when they broke open the atoms, they found they were stuffed with explosions.

While the earth appears to be knowingly keeping its distance from the sun, it really is only centrificating.

One horsepower is how much energy it takes to drag a horse 500 feet in one second.

Rainbows are just for us to look at, but not really understand.

If people run around and around in circles we say that they are crazy. When planets do the same things, we say they are orbiting.

The law of gravity says no fair jumping up without coming back down.

In South America, they have cold summers and hot winters, but somehow they still manage.

There are 26 vitamins in all, but some of the letters haven't been discovered yet. Finding them all means living forever.

Someday we may learn how to make magnets that can point in any direction.

A vibration is a motion that can't make up its mind which way it wants to go.

Lime is a green-tasting rock.

Most books now say that the sun is a star. But it still knows how to change back into a sun in the daytime.

Water freezes at 32 degrees and boils at 212 degrees. There are 180 degrees between boiling and freezing because there are 180 degrees between north and south.

There is a tremendous weight which is pushing down on the center of the earth because of so much population stomping around up there these days.

Many dead animals in the past changed to fossils while others preferred to be oil.

Water vapor gets together in a cloud. When it is big enough to be called a drop, it does.

Clouds just keep circling the earth around and around and around. There is not much else for them to do.

One evening, during a thunderstorm, a mother was tucking her small boy into bed. She was about to leave when he asked, with a tremor in his voice, "Mommy, will you sleep with me tonight?"

"I can't, honey," she said, giving him a hug. "I have to sleep in Daddy's room."

There was a long silence, then he said, "The big sissy!"

A woman doctor was driving her 4-year-old daughter to pre-school. She had left her stethoscope on the car seat and was thrilled when the little girl picked it up and placed it in the proper position. Be still my heart, she thought, My daughter wants to follow in my footsteps. Then the child spoke into the instrument: "Welcome to McDonald's. May I take your order?"

When new people moved in next door, I saw a little girl playing in the yard. I said hello to her and we had a little conversation. "Do you have any brothers or sisters?" I asked. "No," she replied. "I'm the lonely child."

After putting her children to bed, a mother changed into pajama bottoms and an old tshirt and proceeded to wash her hair. The kids, left alone, became rambunctious. So she threw a towel around her head and stormed into their room. "Back to bed, all of you! I mean it!" As she left the room, she heard her youngest say, "Who was that?"

A neighbor was driving with his four-year-old girl, when he accidentally leaned on the horn.

"I did that by accident," he explained to the child in the back.

"I know you did, Daddy."

"How do you know?"

"Because you didn't say, 'JERK!' afterwards."

A little boy opened the big old family Bible and turned the pages. Suddenly, something fell out and he picked it up to examine it. It was an old maple leaf that had been pressed between the pages.

"Mommy!" he called. "Look what I found!"

"What do you have there, sweetie?"

"I think it's Adam's suit!"

I didn't know if my almost-three-year-old granddaughter knew her colors yet; so I tested her. I pointed to various things and she would tell me what color it was; and she was always right. But I was having fun, so I continued with the game, perhaps longer than I should have; because suddenly she headed for the door, saying, "You know, Grandma, I think you should try to figure these out for yourself!"

The three-year-old didn't quite get what marriage was. So her Dad pulled out the wedding photo book and explained every picture. "Now do you understand?" he asked. "I think so," she said. "Is that when Mommy came to work for us?"

While his mother was studying the chapter on hematology for her nursing course, Daniel, four years old, asked what she was reading. Sensing an opportunity to teach, she explained how the heart pumps blood all through our bodies and keeps us alive. Then she taught him to feel the pulse in his wrists and feet.

Daniel wandered off, but his mother noticed him looking at the soles of his feet. He twisted and turned, then pulled down his shorts to look at his bottom. With some difficulty he managed to reach part of his back.

"Whatever are you doing, Danny?"

"Where do we put the batteries?" he asked.

A High School teacher was lecturing his class on why companies advertise and what they do to make people remember them. "That's why companies have slogans," he explained.

"Who can tell me which company says, "I'm lovin' it!"

"McDonald's!" They all knew that one.

"How about 'My baloney has a first name..'"

They knew that one, too. "O-S-C-A-R!"

He mentioned two or three more and discovered his class was pretty savvy about slogans.

"Whose slogan is 'Just do it!'" he asked.

One of the boys quickly shouted out: "My Mom!"

PUNS

PUNS

A sandwich walks into a bar. The bartender says, "We don't serve food here."

Did you hear about the Buddhist who refused his dentist's Novocain during root canal work? He wanted to trandscend dental medication.

I sent ten different puns into a contest, hoping at least one would win. Sadly, no pun in ten did.

A man goes to a psychiatrist complaining of two alternating dreams: "First I'm a wigwam, then I'm a tipi; then I'm a wigwam, then I'm a tipi. What's wrong with me?"

"Simple," says the doctor. "You're two tents."

When she saw her first strands of gray hair, she thought she would dye.

A dyslexic man walks into a bra...

1,000 aches = one megahurtz.

Two peanuts walked into a bar and one was a salted.

An invisible man married an invisible woman. Their kids were nothing to look at either.

When a clock is hungry it goes back four seconds.

Deja moo: the feeling you've heard this bull before.

To write with a broken pencil is pointless.

Hangover: the wrath of grapes.

A bicycle can't stand alone. It's two-tired.

A jumper cable walks into a bar. The bartender says, "I'll serve you, but don't start anything."

The guy who fell into an upholstery machine is fully recovered.

A will is a dead giveaway.

A dentist and a manicurist got married. They fought tooth and nail.

When you've seen one shopping center, you've seen a mall.

A boiled egg is hard to beat.

Dijon vu: the same mustard as before.

Local Area Network in Australia: the LAN down under.

Police were called to a day care center, where a three-year-old was resisting a rest.

Two fish swim into a wall. "Dam!" says one.

A shotgun wedding is a case of wife or death.

A man's home is his castle, in a manor of speaking.

Practice safe eating. Always use condiments.

Does the name Pavlov ring a bell?

The meeting of two egotists: an I for an I.

Santa's helpers are subordinate clauses.

I fired my masseur today. He just rubbed me the wrong way.

Dockyard: a physician's garden.

Oboe: a Cockney tramp.

Toboggan is why we go to an auction.

A pessimist's blood type is always B-negative.

Banning the bra was a big flop.

She criticized my apartment so I knocked her flat.

A 3-legged dog walks into a saloon, saying, "I'm lookin' for the man what shot my paw."

She was arrested after her therapist suggested she take something for her kleptomania.

Two Eskimos sitting in their kayak were chilly so they lit a fire and the boat sank, proving once and for all that you can't heat your kayak and have it too.

Khakis: what you need to start the car in Boston.

When you dream in color, it's a pigment of your imagination.

Reading while sunbathing is sure to make you well red.

Read "How to Handle Overdue Bills" by Jes Burnham.

Condoms should be used on every conceivable occasion.

Incongruous: where bills are passed.

A new kind of broom just came out and it's sweeping the nation.

Alarms: what an octopus is.

Pasteurize: too far to see.

Dancing cheek to cheek is just a form of floor play.

Crick: sound a Japanese camera makes.

A backward poet writes inverse.

A pun is its own reword.

Venetian blind: a sightless Italian.

Famous Viking explorer Leif Ericsson returned home from a voyage and found his name missing on the town register. His wife complained to a local official who apologized profusely, saying, "I must have taken Lief off my census."

Stealing someone's coffee is called mugging.

The electrician got his supplies at the outlet store.

If you wear a blindfold at the shooting range, you won't know what you're missing.

Need an ark to save two of every animal? I noah guy.

Jokes about monorails always make good one-liners.

The book of incantations was useless. The author had failed to run a spell check.

It wasn't that the man didn't know how to juggle. He just didn't have the balls.

Abstinence leaves a lot to be desired.

Organ donors put their heart in it.

When James Bond slept through the earthquake, he was shaken but not stirred.

A group of chess enthusiasts checked into a hotel and stood around in the lobby, discussing their tournament victories. After an hour, the manager came out and asked them to disperse. "I can't stand chess nuts boasting in an open foyer," he explained.

I like to stay current with the electrifying adventures of Sherlock Ohms.

I did a theatrical production about puns. Really, it was just a play on words.

I was going to look for my missing watch but I never could find the time.

A small boy swallowed some coins and was taken to the hospital. When his aunt called for news, the nurse said, "No change yet."

Did you hear about the guy who got hit on the head with a can? Lucky it was a soft drink.

This report is filled with omissions.

A prisoner's favorite punctuation mark is a period, because it marks the end of a sentence.

Cartoonist found dead in home. Details are sketchy.

Never invest in a funeral home. It's a dying industry.

No matter how hard you push the envelope, it's still stationery.

I've been to the dentist many times, so I know the drill.

By definition, one divided by zero is undefined.

King Ozymandius of Assyria was running low on cash after years of war. His last great possession was the Star of the Euphrates, the most valuable diamond in the ancient world. Desperate, he took the diamond to Croesus the pawnbroker. "I'll give you 100,000 dinars for it," said Croesus. "But it's worth millions!" protested the King. "Don't you know who I am? I am your monarch!"

The pawnbroker replied, "When you wish to pawn a Star, makes no difference who you are."

A cow that gives no milk is an udder failure.

Two silk worms had a race. They both ended up in a tie.

Once there were three Indian women. One slept on a deerskin, one on an elkskin and the third, on the skin of a hippopotamus. All three became pregnant. The first two each had a baby boy. The woman who slept on the hippopotamus skin had twin boys.

This just goes to prove that the squaw of the hippopotamus is equal to the sons of the squaws on the other two hides.

An anthropologist was cataloging South American folk remedies with the assistance of a tribal medicine man. When this Brujo said that the leaves of a particular fern were a cure for constipation, the anthropologist scoffed.

The Brujo said, "Let me tell you, with fronds like these, you don't need enemas."

She was only a whisky maker, but he loved her still.

Two hats were hanging on a hat rack in the hallway. One hat said to the other, "You stay here. I'll go on a head."

A dog gave birth to puppies near the highway and was fined for littering.

When cannibals ate a missionary, they got a taste of religion.

Don't join dangerous cults. Practice safe sects!

All the waterfowl kept their eyes closed except one. He was a Peking Duck.

Reassembling the carcass of a prehistoric animal can be a mammoth undertaking.

Gerald thought that if he had to, he could master braille, once he got a feel for it.

Too many spiders in your home can turn it into a no-fly zone.

What did the Mommy tire and the Daddy tire name their little girl tire? Michele Lynn.

I never understood why people like to play softball. It's a very underhanded thing to do.

A noun and a verb were dating but they broke up. The noun was too possessive.

I saw something similar to moss the other day but I didn't know what to lichen it to.

Dogs tend to avoid flea markets.

If it rains cats and dogs, you might step in a poodle.

Where do polar bears vote? The North Poll.

The turkey crossed the road to prove he wasn't chicken.

How to bees get to school? By school buzz.

A fish is easy to weigh because it has its own scales.

A few days after a visit to a house of ill repute, a man noticed green bumps on his genitalia. He hurried to his doctor.

"That's serious," said the doctor. "You've heard that some wrestlers get cauliflower ears?"

"Yes," said the worried man.

"Well," said the doctor, "you've got brothel sprouts."

A Russian couple is walking in Moscow when the man feels a drop hit his nose. "It's raining," he says. "No," says his wife, "It's snow." And they begin to argue. Finally, the man says, "Let's ask Comrade Rudolph what the official weather is."

They approach and ask him. "It is officially raining," he says. The woman cries, "But it felt just like snow!" To which her husband says, "Rudolph the Red knows rain, dear!"

Caterpallor: the color you turn after finding half a worm in the fruit you're eating.

PUNNING ANAGRAMS
(both words use exactly the same letters)

Breasts . . . Bra sets

Debit card . . . Bad credit

Western Union . . . No wire unsent

A decimal point . . . I'm a dot in place

Dormitory . . . Dirty room

Confessional . . .On scale of sin

Geologist . . . Go get oils

Astronomer . . . Moon starer

The eyes . . . They see

The countryside . . . No city dust here

Clint Eastwood . . . Old West action

Astronomers . . . no more stars

Waitress . . . A stew, sir?

Clothespins . . . So let's pinch

Tom Cruise . . . So I'm cuter

Year two thousand . . . a year to shut down

ipod lover . . . poor devil

Conversation . . . Voices rant on

Princess Diana . . . End is a car spin

A shoplifter . . . Has to pilfer

A gentleman . . . Elegant man

Garbage man . . . Bag manager

Christmas . . . Trims cash

Eleven plus two . . . Twelve plus one

Apple, Inc. . . . Epic plan

The United States of America . . . Attaineth its cause: freedom

Statue of Liberty . . . Built to stay free

A telescope . . . To see place

Elvis . . . lives

A frog goes into a bank and approaches one of the service desks. He can see from her nameplate that her name is Patricia Whack.

"Ms. Whack, I'd like to get a $30,000 loan to take a vacation."

Patty looks at the frog in disbelief and asks his name. The frog says his name is Kermit Jagger, his Dad is Mick Jagger and that it's okay, he knows the bank manager.

"Well, okay," says Patty. "But you will need to secure the loan with some collateral.

The frog says, "Sure. I have this," and produces a tiny porcelain elephant, about an inch tall, bright pink, and perfectly formed.

Very confused, Patty explains that she'll have to consult with the bank manager and goes into a back office.

She tells the manager, "There's a frog called Kermit Jagger out there who claims to know you and wants to borrow $30,000, and he wants to use this as collateral." She holds up the tiny pink elephant. "I mean, what in the world is this?"

The bank manager says,

"It's a knickknack, Patty Whack. Give the frog a loan. His old man's a Rolling Stone."

(You're singing it, aren't you? I know you are.)

Testicle: a humorous question on an exam.

Willy-nilly: impotent

Flatulence: emergency vehicle that picks up someone who has been run over by a steamroller.

Glibido: all talk, no action.

Inoculatte: to take coffee intravenously when you are running late.

Decafalon: the grueling event of getting through the day consuming only things that are good for you.

What do you call a plumber with a toilet on his head? Lou.

What do you call a female plumber with two toilets on her head? Lulu.

What do you call someone who used to be called Lee? Formerly.

What would you call a drunk who works at an upholstery shop? A recovering alcoholic.

What's going on when you hear "Woof... splat!...Meow...splat!"
It's raining cats and dogs.

When William signed up with the Army, he disliked the phrase, "Fire at Will."

What does a cow say to the bull? Are you always this horny?

Why can't you play poker in the jungle? Because there are too many cheetahs!

What do eskimos get from sitting around in their igloos too long?
Polaroids!

Laughing stock: cattle with a sense of humor.

Why does a tiger have stripes? So he won't be spotted.

A scientist finally succeeded in cloning himself but the clone only sat around, spewing out filthy jokes and curse words. Finally, the scientist got fed up and pushed the clone out of his 10th-story office window.

A short time later, there was a knock on the office door. The scientist opened the door to find a policeman there, who said, "I'm going to have to arrest you for making an obscene clone fall."

Chickens dance chick to chick.

The undertaker is the last person who will take you down.

An undercover agent is a spy in bed.

VINCENT VAN GOGH'S RELATIVES

His obnoxious brother: Please Gogh!

His dizzy aunt: Verti Gogh

His prune-loving brother: Gotta Gogh

His convenience-store-owner cousin: Stop'n'Gogh

The constipated uncle: Can't Gogh

The ballroom dancer aunt: Tan Gogh

His nephew psychoanalyst: E Gogh

The fruit-loving cousin: Man Gogh

The sister who loved disco: Go Gogh

A bouncy little nephew: Poe Gogh

And his niece who travels the country in an RV: Winnie Bay Gogh

At the annual snail race, the snails were identified by letters on their cars.

As the snail driving the car with the large "S" took the lead, the crowd roared, "Look at that S car go!"

There's nothing like the first horseback ride to make a person feel better off.

I went to a seafood disco last week... and pulled a mussel.

Why is it always hot after baseball games? Because all the fans have left.

Why did the umpire penalize the chicken? For using fowl language.

I was visiting a theme park on an extremely windy day; so I stood inside and looked out to see what, if anything I could do. The park's custodian was a really tiny woman, less than five feet, and slender; and she was having a really tough time trying not to get blown away with the leaves she was attempting to clean up.

I went out and suggested she put rocks into her shoes before she tried to work in such a wind.

"You mean," she said, "Now I weigh me down to sweep?"

A stevedore was in charge of offloading the rice from ships in the harbor. Sadly, the rice was quite moist and did not get sucked up well by the vacuum he was using. He asked his foreman what he should do, and was told, "If at first you don't suck seed, try a drier grain."

While hiking in the woods, Nate and Sam found a huge rock which had an iron lever attached. Etched into the rock were the following words:

"If this lever be pulled, the world will come to an end!"

Nate wanted to pull the lever and see what happened; but Sam was afraid. He told Nate that if he tried to pull the lever, he'd shoot him! Not believing that his friend would do that, Nate lunged for the lever. Sure enough, Sam shot him.

The moral of this story: Better Nate than lever!

Two chefs in Boston were competing for the title of Finest Fish Fryer. They were equally talented and the dishes they created were equally delicious.

However, at the last moment, one of the chefs put a glaze over his entry, and won the title.

"Alas," lamented the other chef. "There but for the glaze of cod go I!"

Snow White took many photos of the 7 dwarfs and their surroundings, so they'd always have something to remember her by. She took her camera into the photo shop and ordered prints enough for each dwarf to have one of each.

The following week, when she went to collect her pictures, the clerk told her that her order had somehow been lost or misplaced. Snow White began to cry. The clerk, to console her, said, "Don't worry, someday your prints will come."

The trouble with other peoples' money is that it's tainted. 'Tain't yours and 'tain't mine.

Customer: I'd like to return this book on modern medical procedures.

Book store owner: Is there something wrong with it?

Customer: Someone removed the appendix.

In 1853, the Tate Watch Company of New Jersey decided to branch out and make new and different products. Tate's Compasses for the pioneers heading West: they would surely be big sellers! But, although they produced fine and accurate watches, the same could not be said of their compasses. Travelers would sometimes end up in Canada or Mexico.

Thus came about the saying, "He who has a Tate's is lost."

A panhandler was caught trying to sneak aboard a Princess cruise ship heading for the Bahamas. He was caught by the Purser who told him: Beggars can't be cruisers!

The U.S. Mint has announced a new fifty-cent piece will be issued. On one side of the coin will be Theodore Roosevelt; on the other, Nathan Hale. Asked why this design had been chosen, the official replied: "Now, when you have a coin toss, you can simply call: "Teds or Hales?"

Once upon a time, there were 3 Kingdoms on the shores of a lake and they all wanted an island in the middle. The three kings decided to have a battle and the winner would take the island. Since this was such a trivial matter, their knights would not fight; the squires would.

The night before the battle, the three different contingents camped on the shores of the lake and readied themselves for battle. The first group had 50 squires; the second group, 20. At the camp of the third kingdom, there was only one knight and his squire. The squire took a large pot, hanging it from a looped rope high in a tree. He cooked a delicious meal in that pot, which he and his knight both enjoyed, then at night lay down in the sand and contemplated the stars.

The other squires were kept busy polishing armor, brushing horses, cooking, cleaning, running and fetching. They got little rest that night.

At the hour of the battle, out went all the squires with their weapons. The battle raged for several hours and when the dust settled, only one person was standing: the lone squire from the third kingdom.

He had defeated the squires from the other two kingdoms, thus proving that the squire of the high pot and noose is equal to the sum of the squires of the other two sides.

Cemetery workers tend to prefer the graveyard shift.

There was a man with a girlfriend named Lorraine. He liked her a lot and even contemplated giving her an engagement ring. And then he met the new girl in town, Clare Lee. She was smart, she was gorgeous, and he wanted her! But how could he dump Lorraine after all the years they had been together? He couldn't.

One day, walking along the river, Lorraine slipped and fell into the river. The swift current carried her off and she sank out of sight.

The man bowed his head for a moment and then stepped off smartly, smiling and singing, "I can see Clare Lee now Lorraine is gone..."

Q: What do chicken families do on Sunday?

A: They go on peck-nics.

Q: What do you get when a chicken lays an egg on the roof of a barn?

A: An egg roll.

Q: Why does a chicken coop have two doors?

A: Because, if it had four doors, it would be a chicken sedan.

Q: How long do chickens work?

A: Around the cluck.

Q: What do chickens serve at birthday parties?

A: Coop-cakes.

NEW WORDS, NEW MEANINGS

INTAXICATION: Euphoria at getting a tax refund, only to realize that it was your money to start with.

KINSTIPATION: The painful inability to get rid of relatives who come to visit.

HEMAGLOBE: The bloody state of the world.

GRANTARTICA: The cold, isolated place where art companies dwell without funding.

BEELZEBUG: Satan in the form of a mosquito that gets into your bedroom during the night and cannot be cast out.

LULLABUOY: An idea that keeps floating into your head and keeps you from drifting off to sleep.

DOPELAR EFFECT: The tendency of stupid Ideas to seem smarter when they come at you rapidly.

BOZONE LAYER: The substance surrounding stupid people that keeps intelligent ideas from penetrating.

FAUNICATION: The destruction of wildlife's natural habitat.

EXTRATERRESTAURANT: Where the food tastes like it came from another planet.

A famous general died and his ashes were set to be taken to Arlington National Cemetery. All the airlines were booked and there were no private planes available. But there was a helicopter, ready to go. It set off and arrived at 6:00 AM at Arlington. The Washington Daily reported the incident with the headline "The Whirly Bird Gets the Urn."

Two contestants on a TV game show were in the final round. Katz was far ahead of Schine; but just as the buzzer went off, Schine slipped ahead and won. When asked what prize he wanted, he said, "A horse." The game show host asked why. "I'll name that horse Harvest Moon," the winner said, "Then I can have a portrait taken, of me on the horse and call it "Schine on Harvest Moon.'"

A news item this morning was about a coal miner, a good amateur painter. He couldn't afford the usual art supplies, so he painted on the walls of his cottage. Yesterday, while he was working, a gang of youths broke into his home and covered his artwork with graffiti. Today, they were charged in court with having corrupted the murals of a miner.

A beautiful snake charmer was wooed by an undertaker and accepted his proposal. At their wedding reception they received many gifts; but their favorite was a set of towels embroidered with the words "Hiss" and "Hearse."

My last job was at Starbucks, but I had to leave because it was always the same old grind.

I tried to be a tailor but I just wasn't suited for it, mostly because it was a sew-sew job.

I gave working at a deli a shot, but any way I sliced it, I couldn't cut the mustard.

I wanted to be a barber but just couldn't cut it.

Working in a muffler factory turned out to be exhausting.

I worked in the woods as a lumberjack, but I just couldn't cut it, so they gave me the ax.

It's hard to understand how a cemetery raised its burial cost and blamed it on the cost of living.

Did you know William Tell and his family were avid bowlers? It's true. But unfortunately, a fire destroyed all the league records. So we'll never know for whom the Tells bowled.

What time is it when it's time to go to the dentist? Tooth hurty.

Why did the golfer wear two pairs of pants? In case he got a hole in one.

Two mushrooms walk into a bar. They sit down and order drinks. The bartender says, "We don't serve mushrooms here." "Why not?" says one. "We're fun guy."

Two boll weevils grew up in Alabama. One went to Hollywood and became a famous actor. The other stayed behind in the cotton fields and never amounted to much. The second one, naturally, became know as the lesser of two weevils.

This guy goes into a restaurant for breakfast on Christmas Day because it advertises Special Christmas Breakfast. He orders Eggs Benedict. His order comes served on a big shiny hubcap. "What's this?" he asks. The waiter says, "There's no plate like chrome for the hollandaise."

A doctor had a regular habit of stopping off at his favorite bar for a hazelnut daiquiri. The bartender knew him and would always have the drink waiting at precisely 5:03 PM. One afternoon, the bartender was dismayed to find that he had no hazelnuts in the place but he had other nuts. He chose hickory and made a drink with it. The doctor came in at his regular time, took a sip, and exclaimed: "This isn't a hazelnut daiquiri!"

"No, I'm sorry," replied the bartender. "It's a hickory daiquiri, Doc."

Two people in an ambulance? Pair o' medics.

Not only has Origami Bank folded, but Sumo Bank has gone belly up and Bonsai Bank plans to cut back some of its branches. Karaoke Bank is up for sale and is (you guessed it) going for a song.

A hungry lion roaming through the jungle came upon two men. One was sitting in a tree, reading a book; the other, on the ground, was pounding away on his laptop. The lion quickly pounced on the man reading the book and devoured him. Even the King of the Jungle knows readers digest and writers cramp.

He used to work in a blanket factory, but it folded.

Is a book on voyeurism a peeping tome?

A gossip is someone with a great sense of rumor.

He often broke into song because he couldn't find the key.

Why can a man never starve in the Mohave Desert? Because he can eat the sand which is there. But what brought the sandwiches there? Why Noah sent Ham, and his descendants mustered and bred.

Sea Captains don't like crew cuts.

Ray was discharged from the Marines because he was rotten to the Corps.

To err is human; to moo, bovine.

Two banks with different rates have a conflict of interest.

Without geometry, life is pointless.

Then there was the man who bought a cattle ranch for his sons and called it the Focus Ranch because it was where the sons raise meat. (three punning words)

Many years ago, a baker's assistant called Richard the Pourer (because his job was to pour the batter for the sausage roll into the pan) noticed he was running low on some spice he needed. He sent his apprentice to the store.

Unfortunately, upon entering the shop, the apprentice realized he'd forgotten the name of the spice. All he could do was to tell the shopkeeper that it was for Richard the Pourer, for batter for wurst.

Those who get too big for their britches will be exposed in the end.

Stalemate: a leading cause of divorce.

Never judge a book by its author

Book Title	Author
Animal Illnesses	Ann Thrax
Population Growth in France	Francis Crowded
Keeping up with Underwear	Lucy Lastic
Handel's Messiah	Ollie Luyah
Irish Flooring	Lynn O'leum
Cloning	Ima Dubble
I Lived in Detroit	Helen Earth
Inflammation, Please	Arthur Itis
Avoiding High Building Costs	Bill Jerome Home
What Lonely Gals Should Do	Seymour Fellows
Leo Tolstoy	Warren Peace
L.A. Lakers' Breakfast	Kareem O'Wheat
Neither a Borrower	Nora Linda Bee
The French Chef	Sue Flay
The Scent of a Man	Jim Nazlum
Tight Situation	Leah Tard
Look Younger	Faye Slift
How I Made Money	Robin Banks
Car Trouble	M.T. Tank
And Shut Up!	Sid Downe
No!	Kurt Reply
Wind in the Willows	Russell Ingleaves
Mountain Climbing	Andover Hand

I relish the fact that you've mustard the strength to ketchup to me.

Double negatives are a no-no.

I knew a guy who became addicted to soap. He's clean now.

John Deere's manure spreader is the only equipment the company won't stand behind.

A hungry traveler stops at a monastery and is taken to the kitchens. A brother is frying potatoes.

"Are you the cook?" the traveler asks. "No, I'm the chip monk."

Greengrocers earn a meager celery, come home beet and just want to read the pepper, take a leek, turnip the covers, endive into bed.

A pencil could be made with erasers at both ends... but what would be the point?

I've been to the dentist several times, so I know the drill.

It was an emotional wedding. Even the cake was in tiers.

DAFT DEFINITIONS

DAFT DEFINITIONS

CHICKENS: the only animal you eat before they are born and after they are dead.

CANNIBAL: someone who is fed up with people.

HANDKERCHIEF: cold storage

COMMITTEE: a body of people that keeps minutes and wastes hours.

TOMORROW: one of the greatest labor-saving devices of today.

HARD WATER: ice

NITRATE: much cheaper than a day rate.

FIBULA: a little lie.

VARICOSE: close by

YAWN: an honest opinion, openly expressed.

VULNERABLE: (female) Opening up completely to another person. (male) Playing football without a cup.

COMMITMENT: (female) Finding your one true love and getting married. (male) Trying not to hit on other women while out with this one.

REMOTE CONTROL: (female) A device for changing channels on the television. (male) A device that can scan through all 175 channels in under five minutes.

DUST: mud with the juice squeezed out.

RAISIN: grape with a sunburn

INFLATION: cutting money in half without damaging the paper.

MOSQUITO: an insect that makes you appreciate flies.

WRINKLES: something other old people have ... similar to my character lines.

CANTELOUPE: gotta get married in church.

IMMEDIATE: to refrain from meditating.

CLOTHES DRYER: an appliance that eats socks.

SEASON: male offspring of Poseidon

LIQUOR: how a male animal cleans his mate.

MARITIME: the hour of a wedding.

SYNONYM: a linguist's favorite spice.

MEDIEVAL: not completely wicked.

THESAURUS: a dinosaur that knows a lot of words.

ABDICATE: to give up all hope of ever having a flat stomach.

TUMOR: one more than one more.

PARASITES: what you see from the top of the Eiffel Tower.

URINE: where you are when you aren't out.

RECTUM: nearly killed 'em.

ABASEMENT: where the furnace is.

BUCCANEER: what pirates are paying for corn these days.

HUMDINGER: the sound a grandfather clock makes just before striking.

AFTERMATH: relaxation after algebra class.

OXYMORON: as dumb as an ox.

INFANTRY: a young, immature tree.

MALEDICTION: the way men talk.

ACRE: someone with aches and pains.

BIDE: past tense of buy.

CAUTERIZE: made eye contact with her.

GOAD: past tense of go.

OCTOPUS: eight-legged cat.

BACTERIA: the back door of the cafeteria.

MEDICAL STAFF: a cane for the doctor.

NODE: past tense of know.

PARADOX: two physicians.

TABLET: a small table.

BALONEY: where some skirt hemlines fall.

BURGLARIZE: what some crooks see with.

FLATULENCE: emergency vehicle that picks you up after you are run over by a steamroller.

CORONER: a round corner

PRIMATE: removing your mate from in front of the television.

MYTH: a female moth.

PHARMACIST: helper on the farm.

NORMALIZE: 20/20 vision.

SEALS: animals you find on legal documents.

DIODE: a pair of two long poems.

EGOTIST: someone me-deep in conversation.

OILY: the opposite of late.

POLARIZE: what penguins see with.

POLYGON: a dead parrot.

TOOTHACHE: a pain that drives you to extraction.

SUBDUED: a guy who, like, works on one of those, like, submarines.

SELFISH: what the seafood store sells.

ACCOUNT: husband of a countess.

BENIGN: what you be after you be eight.

ASSET: a little donkey.

INOCULATTE: taking coffee intravenously.

PHONY: related to telephones.

CROAKROOM: where tadpoles go to change.

THINGY: (female) any part under a car's hood. (male) the fastener on a woman's bra.

ANAGRAM PUNS: same letter in both words

COMFORT IS: MICROSOFT

JAY LENO: ENJOY L.A.

THE TITANIC DISASTER: DEATH, IT STARTS IN ICE.

TELEVISION PROGRAMMING: PERMEATING LIVING ROOMS

FUNERAL: REAL FUN

STATUE OF LIBERTY: BUILT TO STAY FREE

A SHOPLIFTER: HAS TO PILFER

HEROES: what a guy in a boat does.

SHORTENING: one of the important ingredients in a good sermon.

CONTROL: a short, ugly inmate.

HANGNAIL: what you put your coat on.

ACCRUE: the people who run a sailboat.

BERNADETTE: the act of torching the mortgage.

AVOIDABLE: what the bullfighter tries to do.

ACOUSTIC: a long pole used to play pool.

ARBITRATOR: a cook who leaves Arby's to work for McDonald's.

BARIUM: what we do to most people after they have died.

LEFT BANK: what the robber did when his bag was full of loot.

SECRET: something you tell to only one person at a time.

SKELETON: a bunch of bones with the person scraped off.

BULLDOZER: a sleeping bull

ADULT: a person who has stopped growing up at both ends and is now growing in the middle.

MILK DUD: a cow that won't give milk.

BISON: what the buffalo said to his child when he left on a trip.

SPOILED MILK: what you get from a pampered cow.

SOUTHPAW: a dog who is left-handed.

FLABBERGASTED: appalled by how much weight one has gained.

HEIR RAID: when the relatives gather to hear the reading of the will.

HATCHET: what a hen does to an egg.

GOSSIP: information that goes in both ears and comes out of the moth greatly enlarged.

OLD TIMER: one who rememers when the moon inspired romance, not space travel.

GIRAFFITI: spray painting very very high.

KARMAGEDDON: when all the Hippies blow up together.

HENCE: an enclosure around a chicken yard.

CADILLAC: missing cattle.

BAND-AID: a fund to help a band.

BABYSITTER: a small child who hasn't yet learned to crawl or walk.

DOG PADDLE: a rolled-up newspaper used to train a puppy.

MOTH BALL: a social event for moths.

PUT-DOWN: too hot to handle.

QUARTERBACK: change you get when you buy a 75-cent item with a dollar bill.

MEGAPHONE: a very large telephone.

MATCHBOOK: a novel about matches.

REMIND: a brain transplant.

INSTALLMENT: putting a horse into its stall.

OLDHAM: a town in England where they make awful sandwiches.

What do you call a New York manufacturer of men's headwear? Manhattan.

What do you call a Mexican man who lost his car? Carlos.

POLITICALLY CORRECT WAYS TO DESCRIBE MEN

He is not short; he is vertically challenged.

He is not balding; he is in advanced follicle regression.

He doesn't have a huge beer belly; he has developed a portable liquid malt and hops storage facility.

He is not stupid; he suffers from minimal cranial development.

He does not get lost; he discovers alternative destinations.

He does not get falling-down drunk; he becomes involuntarily horizontal.

He doesn't hog the blankets; his is thermally unappreciative.

He is not a male chauvinist pig; he has grunt-hog empathy.

He does not eat like a pig; he suffers from reverse bullemia.

A speech is like a bicycle wheel; the longer the spoke, the greater the tire.

A volcano is just a mountain with hiccups.

Why do you need a winter coat to wax the car? Because the container says a heavy coat makes the shine last longer.

Theft in Beijing: Chinese takeaway

OUTFIT: pitching a fit outdoors.

LIFE JACKET: a coat that will last a lifetime.

LAUGHINGSTOCK: cattle, horses, sheep and hogs responding to a really good joke.

HIMALAYA: a rooster who lays an egg.

IDEAL PERSON: a person who insists upon dealing every hand.

REFUSE: replacing a burnt-out fuse.

ILLEGAL: a sick bird.

NETWORK: the process of making nets.

ROMAN: a person who doesn't stay in one place very long.

WRITER: one who corrects a wrong.

VITAMIN: what you do when someone comes to the house.

WORKOUT: a job outdoors.

CLASS ACTION: a stylish deed.

SEASON: male offspring of Poseidon.

SYNTAX: a tariff on immorality.

MARITIME: hour when the wedding will start.

EXERCISE: her former body measurements.

ACRE: Someone who aches.

LIQUOR: how a male animal cleans his mate.

GOOD-BYE: a bargain.

ARTERY: a place where they keep paintings.

THESAURUS: a dinosaur that eats its words.

PROFESSOR: the opposite of confessor.

LABOR PAIN: the result of a work injury.

TERMINAL ILLNESS: an airport sickness.

SEIZURE: a Roman emperor with epilepsy.

HANDICAP: a head covering that is easy to locate.

DEFILE: remove from alphabetical order.

BARBARIAN: related to Barbara.

ABASEMENT: where you'll find the furnace.

MALEDICTION: the way men talk.

DETAIL: taking off an animal's tail.

HIGH SCHOOL: a school on top of the Empire State Building.

COOKOUT: the cook's day off.

GOSSIP: 24-hour teller

SWEATER: a person who freely perspires.

TIMEKEEPER: that guy who never returned your watch.

WELL DONE: now you have running water.

OUTPATIENT: a person who has fainted.

MORBID: a higher offer.

DILATE: to live a long long life.

PHONY: related to telephones.

SILVERFISH: a precious fish, not quite as expensive as a goldfish.

POSTOPERATIVE: the mailman.

PHARMACIST: a helper on the farm.

POLITE: a lamp on a pole.

POLYGON: The parrot that got away.

LIP SERVICE: putting lipstick on someone else.

PIGGYBACK: the lost hog is back home.

UNDERCOVER AGENT: a spy in bed.

UNABATED: a fishhook without a worm.

VERTIGO: directions in Germany

TRAVELER'S AID: a soft drink in the bus station.

TUBA: a compound word: "Hey, bring me another tuba toothpaste!"

TUMOR: an extra pair.

TUNER: a popular fish, often served from the can.

VICE VERSA: erotic Italian poetry.

VILIFICATION: the inexorable spread of Greenwich Village.

WEAK-KNEED: seven days required.

WEIGHTLESS: your diet worked!

WEIGHTLESS (alt.): a shorter wait.

WARDEN: the video game room.

WINDOW: what all gamblers want to do.

ABASH: a great party.

ACQUIT: I've had enough!

ACAPULCO: music sung without accompaniment.

ADMINISTER: increasing the clergy.

AUTOMATED: a couple making love in a car.

BARD: past tense of "to borrow" in the South.

BASHFUL: harsh and abusive.

BAR: what a Southerner hunts in the woods.

BARREN: a naked bird.

CAMELOT: where to shop for a dromedary.

BUSH PILOT: flew Air Force One.

CANCER: cure for smoking.

BOUYANT: male insect.

CATACLYSM: religious study for felines.

CARPE DIEM: gripe of the day.

CATATONIC: what feline bars mix with vodka.

CHASTE: why virgins run.

CONTRITE: the lament of illiterates.

CHAIN GANG: guys in a bar wearing too much gold jewelry.

CLEAVAGE: something which you can approve of and look down on.

DARE: not here.

DAZE: opposite of knights.

DEATH: something you can live without.

DISBELIEF: how you describe the green stuff on a tree.

DONATION: a country of female deer.

EASTER: not as far West.

ERECTION: when the Japanese vote.

EX-LAX: formerly the Los Angeles airport.

GROUNDHOG: sausage.

GRAVITY: not just a good idea, it's the law.

CHOPPED CABBAGE: not just a good idea, it's the slaw.

PIGMENT: mint grown to feed hogs.

OZONE: erogenous area.

PARAFFINS: found on the sides of fish.

PARALYZE: "Of course I'll love you tomorrow" and "The check's in the mail."

OVA: finished; done with.

OUTPUT: what Yoda does with his cat.

OPAL: Hi, buddy!

NAUTICAL: don't tickle me!

MUNCHKIN: what cannibals do with their relatives.

MUSHROOM: place where couples neck.

MONOGAMY: leaves a lot to be desired.

AFTERMATH: period following algebra class.

AIR POLLUTION: mist demeanor.

AMIDST: foggy.

BARBAROUS: a bad haircut.

BAGELS: birds that live near a bay.

BELITTLE: the imperative form of shrink.

CABBAGE: the number of years a taxi has existed.

CAMPUS: show us where to pitch our tent.

CISTERN: opposite of brethren.

CLASS ACTION: a stylish deed.

CRIBBAGE: when you are a baby.

BOUNTY HUNTER: seeker of paper towels.

COPULATE: what the Italian police chief says to an officer who isn't on time.

DAMNATION: the country of beavers.

DECAY: de letter dat comes after de Jay.

ENLIST: n, n, n, n, n, n, n, n, n, n, n, n, n, n, n, n

EN MASSE: a very large Church service.

LOCOMOTIVE: crazy reason.

LOG ON: make the fire hotter.

LOG OFF: don't add any more wood.

LUTE: money.

MAIDEN: where bears sleep after April is over.

LUCILLE: aquarium escapee.

LUMBAR PUNCTURE: a hole in a 2 by 4.

MAY: a month when you might.

MASSEURS: people who knead people.

OPERETTA: the lady who says, "Number, please."

OPTICS: bugs with very good eyesight.

PLANT MANAGER: gardener.

PLEA BARGAIN: a good price on fresh pleas.

POKER: dig her in the ribs.

FAR: a conflagration in Alabama.

FEAST: an eat wave.

FORFEIT: what most animals stand on.

GIGOLO: a fee male.

GIRL SCOUT: a boy looking out for females.

HATE CRIME: who doesn't?

INTESTINE: currently taking an exam.

IOTA: a Toyota with payments still due.

KIBBLE: one thousand nibbles.

KNAPSACK: sleeping bag.

KNOT HOLE: only partial.

NEW AGE: what a girl gives instead of her real age.

NIGHTMARE: a female horse used only in the evening.

OBESITY: surplus gone to waist.

HARRASS: her rear end.

HAWAIIAN GARLAND: the lei of the land.

HIGH FIDELITY: a drug addict who always goes home to his wife.

HERNIA: pertaining to the female knee.

INCISOR: person who exercises indoors.

IMPECCABLE: unable to be eaten by a chicken.

LATENT: French camping shelter.

LIGHT YEAR: a year with fewer calories.

LIVER: one who isn't dead.

OFFLINE: failure to pass a sobriety test.

PECAN: a container to urinate in.

PERVERSE: a poem about a cat.

POLITICS: that parrot has swallowed a watch.

PRAISE: letting off esteem.

PRO BONO: in favor of Sonny.

PROFOUND: we discovered an expert!

RABBIT: small portion of a rabbi.

RATIFY: to use a spell and turn someone into a rat.

REFINED: locate again.

RELAY: make love a second time.

RESERVE: offering seconds at dinner.

REST STOP: traffic light stuck on red.

RINGWORM: worm with a bell.

ROCK MUSIC: sung in a rocking chair.

ROUTINE: dental work.

RUBBER BAND: flexible musicians.

SCORE PAD: a bachelor's apartment.

SCAR: rolled tobacco leaf.

SANDWICH: beach Wiccan.

SECURITY: what guards drink.

SECRETION: the act of hiding something.

SALT: something useful in a pinch.

SNUFF: sufficient unto the day.

SOLO: location of the hem on a long skirt.

SONOGRAM: a telegram from your son.

SOUL MAN: a cobbler.

SUBSIDY: a town beneath another town.

STAGNATION: a country of single men.

TABLET: a small table.

SURGEON: a doctor on the cutting edge.

SWEET SIXTEEN: just down the hall from Suite 14.

TAUT: educated.

TAX: a fine for doing fine.

TANGENT: a man who's been in the sun.

TELEPATHY: minding someone else's business.

TIRELESS: have a car but no wheels.

TOAD: what happens to an illegally parked frog.

ULTRASOUND: any very loud noise.

UNICORN: one-of-a-kind maize.

URINAL: a place where all men are peers.

VEIN: conceited.

WIND: like air, only pushier.

YOKE: Swedish humor.

ZEBRA: ze cloth that covers ze bosom.

YANKEE: same as a quickie, but you do it by yourself.

BEELZEBUG: a mosquito you can't get rid of.

DEJA-STEW: leftovers.

ESPRESSO: very fast coffee.

MEANDERTHAL: a very slow caveman.

OSTEOPORNOSIS: a degenerate disease.

MOOSES: Hebrew prophet of the Maine woods.

LAMBPOON: to make fun of sheep.

JEANEOLOGY: the study of Levi's, Wrangler's, and other denims.

UNTOLD WEALTH: what you left out on April 15th.

UNDERMINE: relative position...there's an apartment undermine.

URINE: You made it!

VIOLIN: a bad hotel.

YALE: Norwegian prison.

TREASON: what the acorn is to the oak.

YES-MEN: those who obey the man nobody no's.

SUDSICLE: ice-cold beer.

SARCHASM: the gulf between the sarcastic wit and the person who doesn't get it.

PROCATSTINATE: when the cat can't decide to stay in or go out.

TUNAR: sonar-like device that causes cats to appear.

TATYR: a lecherous Mr. Potato Head.

WEELIEF: the feeling one gets upon spotting a rest area on the highway.

XENAPHOBIA: fear of warrior princesses.

ACOUSTIC: instrument used to play pool.

ACUTE: opposite of an ugly.

WARSHIP: adoration of the Navy.

BELITTLE: the imperative form of shrink.

DODO: a double negative with a head cold.

DOGMA: a puppy's mother

WEDDING RING: a one-man band.

EJACULATE: Jill telling her boyfriend he's tardy again.

ESCAPE: one size larger than an "'R" cape.

EXPRESS: formerly of print media.

EXPELLED: used to be a witch

FORPAWS: a moment of silence before a golfer tees off.

TANGENT: a man who's been in the sun.

TAR (Southern U.S.): a rubber wheel.

LAD: a short ladder.

LACTIC: the clock doesn't work.

KIT 'N' KABOODLE: a whole lot of cats.

LINGO: one of the Japanese Beatles.

LEGAL BRIEFS: the lawyer's shorts.

LOCOMOTIVE: crazy reason for one's actions.

JOCULAR: of or pertaining to sports.

KETCHUP: what slow runners are always trying to do.

JUDO: currency of Israel.

INTERNET SCAM: dot con.

INTESTINES: beta versions of forks.

IRONY: metallurgical.

MALPRACTICE: shopping until you get it right.

MALCONTENT: you got it right and you're happy.

MEGABYTE: a nine-course dinner.

NEIGHBORHOOD: a felon who lives near you.

PLATELET: a saucer.

PLANKTON: about 2,000 pounds of lumber.

GAUCHO: the Marx Brothers' Mexican cousin.

FORESKIN: between 3-skin and 5-skin.

MAMMOGRAM: a telegram to Mommy.

SIGNS, BILLBOARDS

& BUMPER STICKERS

SIGNS, BILLBOARDS & BUMPER STICKERS

In a restaurant window: OPEN 7 DAYS A WEEK AND WEEKENDS.

In a ladies' restroom in Texas: WOMAN'S RULE OF THUMB: if it has tires or testicles, you're going to have trouble with it.

An Ikea billboard: Come check out our stool samples.

On a billboard: We're proud of our privates. United States Army

On a doctor's office in Rome, Italy: Specialist in Women and Other Diseases

Dry cleaner sign, Bangkok: Drop Your Trousers Here for Best Results

On a car bumper: Dyslexics, untie!

Cows, never bred. Also for sale: gay bull.

Sign in a hotel in Japan: You are invited to take advantage of the chambermaid

Bumper sticker: Forgive your enemy but remember the bastard's name.

Sign in a bar: Alcohol does not solve any problem. But then, neither does milk.

Ladies' room, Delray Beach, Florida: Friends don't let friends take home ugly men.

Written in the dust on the back of a bus: It's hard to make a comeback when you haven't been anywhere.

Sign over the urinals in a bar: Express Lane: five beers or less

Sign over the sink mirror, same bar: No wonder you always go home alone

Newspaper headline: Man Kills Self Before Shooting Wife and Daughter

Another newspaper headline: Red Tape Holds Up New Bridges

It's all about the bitches. U.S.Kennel Club

Need a good screw? Ace Hardware

Want to earn money hand over fist? Call us: Cryogenic Sperm Bank

Daisy Air Rifles: Keeping Kids Off Your Lawn Since 1886

Like her mugs? You should see her cans. St. Pauli Girl beer

Dude, we totally forgot our slogan. American Medical Marijuana Association

In a men's room: No matter how good she looks, some other guy is sick of her crap.

In a ladies' room: Make love, not war. Hell, do both! Get married!

Over the mirror in a rest room: You're too good for him!

Bumper sticker: IN DOG YEARS, I'm dead!

Bumper sticker: I'm retired. I was tired yesterday and I'm tired again today.

FREE DOG. Hateful little bastard. Bites!

Notice in a field: the farmer allows walkers to cross the field, but the bull charges.

In the toilet of a London office: TOILET OUT OF ORDER. PLEASE USE FLOOR BELOW.

In a house: I only have a kitchen because it came with the house.

In another house: I'm not 40-something. I'm 39.95 plus shipping & handling.

In a third house: I don't have hot flashes. I have short, private vacations in the Tropics.

On a cardiologist's wall: What fits your busy schedule better–exercising one hour a day or being dead 24 hours a day?

In a small-town newspaper: Get 50% off or half price, whichever is less.

News headline: Federal Agents Raid Gun Shop, Find Weapons.

In the Personals Section: TOMBSTONE FOR SALE. Standard gray color. Good for someone named Grady.

Sign in Seoul: PLEASE DO NOT FEED FISH WITH YOUR PRIVATE.

Tshirt: You say psycho like it's a bad thing.

In a small-town newspaper: FOR SALE: Complete set of Encyclopedia Brittanica, 45 volumes, excellent condition. $1,000 or best offer. No longer needed. Got married last weekend and find that my wife knows absolutely everything!

Sign on a Bangkok fence:

All of you listen to mee. Don't disturb here. I will call Police catch you. Don't come to my bangalow house, understand, OK. I hate all of you.

Hangtag on man's shirt in China:
WASH BY HAND 30 C.
NO CHLORINE
NO WRING
IN COLESLAW

Sign in a Thai hotel: CAUTION. When you take a bath, please close the door and switch on the fun without fail.

At another hotel:

Dear guests, We are now start cleaning the hotel walls, outside part, which is part of the building painting process. The workers will hang themselves from the top of the hotel down to the ground. They also have to hang themselves outside your balcony. This may cause you inconvenience during your stay. The hotel management would like to apologise for the inconvenience. Thank you.

Outside zoo in India: Please do not Annoy, Torment, Pester, Molest, Worry, Badger, Harry, Harass, Hackle, Persecute, Irk, Rag, Vex, Bother, Tease, Nettle, Tantalise or Ruffle the Animal.

On a tshirt: ELVIS IS DEAD. SINATRA IS DEAD. And ME I feel also not so good

In the personals: WEDDING DRESS FOR SALE Worn once by mistake.

Another one: JOINING NUDIST COLONY! Must sell washer and dryer. Only $200!

FREE PUPPIES. Mother is a Kennel Club registered German Shepherd. Father is Super Dog, able to leap tall fences in a single bound.

On the main road to Mombassa, leaving Nairobi: TAKE NOTICE. WHEN THIS SIGN IS UNDER WATER, THIS ROAD IS IMPASSABLE.

In a cemetery: PERSONS ARE PROHIBITED FROM PICKING FLOWERS FROM ANY BUT THEIR OWN GRAVES.

Cocktail lounge, Norway: LADIES ARE REQUESTED NOT TO HAVE CHILDREN IN THE BAR.

DYSLEXICS HAVE MORE NUF!

On a poster: ARE YOU AN ADULT THAT CANNOT READ? IF SO, WE CAN HELP.

On the menu of a Swiss restaurant: OUR WINES LEAVE YOU NOTHING TO HOPE FOR.

Hotel in Zurich: Because of the impropriety of entertaining guests of the opposite sex in the bedroom, it is suggested that the lobby be used for this purpose.

In the lobby of a Moscow hotel opposite a Russian Orthodox church:
YOU ARE WELCOME TO VISIT THE CEMETERY WHERE FAMOUS RUSSIAN AND SOVIET COMPOSERS, ARTISTS AND WRITERS ARE BURIED DAILY EXCEPT THURSDAY.

Sign for donkey rides, Thailand: WOULD YOU LIKE TO RIDE ON YOUR OWN ASS?

Tokyo hotel rule: GUESTS ARE REQUESTED NOT TO SMOKE OR DO OTHER DISGUSTING BEHAVIOURS IN BED.

In a Roman laundry: LADIES, LEAVE YOUR CLOTHES HERE AND SPEND THE AFTERNOON HAVING A GOOD TIME.

Tokyo bar sign: SPECIAL COCKTAILS FOR THE LADIES WITH NUTS.

SOME BUMPER STICKERS WE'VE SEEN

4 out of 5 voices in my head say GO FOR IT!

Answer my prayer...Steal this car!

Back off! I'm a Postal worker!

CAUTION: legally Blonde!

Clear the road! I'm SIXTEEN!

Don't follow me. I'm lost.

Forget about World Peace. Visualize using your turn signal!

I may be slow, but I'm ahead of you.

I brake for tailgaters!

I'm a nice guy, but my car is evil.

I'm Out of Estrogen and I Have a Gun!

If you can read this, I've lost my trailer.

THE EARTH IS FULL. GO HOME!

So many pedestrians, so little time!

Life is short. PRAY HARD.

My road to success is under construction.

I'll keep my guns, my money and my health care. You keep the change.

This vehicle STOPS at all garage sales!

DON'T LAUGH... IT'S PAID FOR.

SORRY! This is as fast as this thing will go!

COME TO THE DARKSIDE. We have cookies.

I had a life...My job ate it!

My DOG is my CO-PILOT.

LOVE THY NEIGHBOR. Just don't get caught.

Well-behaved women rarely make history.

FEMINISM: THE RADICAL NOTION THAT WOMEN ARE HUMAN BEINGS

Jewish pagans are like regular pagans. We believe in the Mother Goddess but we feel guilty about not calling.

BEER IS TECHNICALLY A VEGETARIAN MEAL

Sign in a pet shop: Buy a dog, get many fleas.

NO TRESPASSING. VIOLATORS WILL BE SHOT. SURVIVORS WILL BE SHOT AGAIN.

In the Everglades: PEOPLE WHO THROW OBJECTS AT THE CROCODILES WILL BE ASKED TO RETRIEVE THEM

Billboard: We're proud of our organs. HAMMOND

Another billboard: Sexism hurts everyone... especially broads

And another: There is life after substance abuse. It's just not particularly fun.

CANADA: leading the world in being just North of the United States

Sign in a Korean park: TODAY IS UNDER CONSTRUCTION. THANK YOU FOR UNDERSTANDING.

Highway sign: PLEASE. Neuter your pets. And weird friends and relatives.

Kentucky: Five million people. Fifteen last names.

REAL TRUE ACTUAL CLASSIFIED ADS

Amana washer $100. Owned by clean bachelor who seldom washed.

Snow blower for sale...only used on snowy days.

Free puppies...part German Shepherd part Dog

2 wire mesh butchering gloves, 1 5-finger, 1 3-finger, PAIR: $15

Tickle Me Elmo, still in box, comes with its own 1988 Mustang, 5L, auto, excellent condition $6800

'83 Toyota Hunchback -- $2000

Star Wars Job Of The Hut -- $15

Free puppies: part Cocker Spaniel - part sneaky neighbor's dog

Soft & genital bath tissues or facial tissue - 89 cents

German Shepherd. 85 lbs. Neutered. Speaks German. Free.

Free 1 can of pork & beans with purchase of 3 br 2 bth home. Sale: Lee Majors (6 million $ man) - $50

Nordic Track $300 - hardly used - call Chubbie

Bill's Septic Cleaning - "We haul American made products"

Shakespeare's Pizza - free chopsticks

Found: dirty white dog...looks like a rat...been out awhile...better be reward.

Hummels - largest selection ever - "If it's in stock, we have it!"

Get a little john: the traveling urinal - holds 2 bottles of beer.

Harrisburg Postal Employees Gun Club

Georgia Peaches - California grown - 89 cents lb.

Nice parachute - never opened - used once - slightly stained

Free: farm kittens. Ready to eat.

American Flag - 60 stars - pole included - $100

Tired of working for only $9.75 per hour? We offer profit sharing and flexible hours. Starting pay: $7 - $9 per hour.

Exercise equipment: Queen size mattress & box spring -$175.

Notice: To person or persons who took the large pumpkin on highway 87 near Southridge Storage. Please return the pumpkin and be checked. Pumpkin may be radioactive. All other plants in vicinity are dead.

Our sofa seats the whole mob - and it's made of 100% Italian leather.

Alzheimer's center prepares for an affair to remember

Ground Beast: 99 cents lb.

Bar S Sliced Bologna - regular or tasty - save 30 cents on 2

Open house - body shapers toning salon - free coffee & donuts

Money is like manure. It's no good unless it's spread around.

I wasn't going to do anything today. So far, I'm right on schedule.

Housework won't kill you...but why take the chance?

LAUNDRY ROOM. PUSH BUTTON FOR SERVICE. If no one answers, do it yourself.

My house was clean last week...sorry you missed it.

I SERVE 3 MEALS: FROZEN, MICROWAVE & TAKE-OUT

DOUBLE JEOPARDY: when a woman teaches another woman to drive.

Seen posted in a ladies' room: My boyfriend has a 30-year mortgage, a 5-year car lease and a lifetime gym membership. And he's afraid to commit!!

LIFE IS MADE OF CHOICES. REMOVE YOUR SHOES OR SCRUB THE FLOOR.

Newspaper headline: Fish need water, Feds say.

Another one: Alton attorney accidentally sues self.

And another: County pays $25,000 to advertise lack of funds

How about this one: Utah Poison Control Center reminds everyone not to take poison

Or: Caskets found as workers demolish mausoleum

Sign at a hotel in Beijing:

EXTERIOR WINDOW CLEANERS AT WORK!
NO FEEDING!

NEWSPAPER CLIPPINGS FROM ALL OVER

The Learning Center reports that a man across the way stands at his window for hours, staring at the children. Police have ID'ed the subject as a cardboard cutout of Arnold Schwartzenegger.

WANTED: Somebody to go back in time with me. This is not a joke. P.O Box 322, Oakview, CA 93022. You'll get paid after we get back. Must bring your own weapons. Safety not guaranteed. I have only done this once before.

From a Michigan weekly: Police checked the area and found an open door in the back of the building. An officer went inside and called out, "Marco!" Police found the suspect when he answered, "Polo!"

Lower Duck Pond, Lithia Park, Ashland–Police responded to a report of two dogs running loose and attacking ducks at about 11:20 AM Sunday. The officer cited a resident for the loose dogs. The duck refused medical attention and left the area, according to police records.

5 PM–Police were called to Market Square for a report about a "suspicious coin." Investigating officer reported it was a quarter.

FOR SALE: HUMAN SKULL. USED ONCE ONLY. Not plastic. $200 OBO.

Dolores Castro said she likes shopping at the Dollar Store because it is convenient and casual. "I don't like to get all dressed up like I'm going to Wal-Mart or something," she said.

ARMY VEHICLE DISAPPEARS An Australian Army vehicle worth $75,000 has gone missing after being painted with camouflage.

QUESTION OF THE DAY:
Q: What constitutes a millionaire?
A: A millionaire is someone who has $1million, according to a senior vice president of investments at RG Klein and Sons.

Sign in an optometrist's window: If you don't see what you want, you've come to the right place.

In a will: Being of sound mind, I spent all my money before I died.

Notice in a public park flower garden: "Love 'em and leave 'em."

License plate on car of drill sergeant: HUP 234

Sign on a country road: If you're lost, just keep on going. You're making good time.

In an art gallery: We hung these pictures because we couldn't find the artists.

CHURCH BULLETINS (none made up)

Don't let worry kill you off. Let the Church help.

Miss Mary Jane Jones sang, "I Will Not Pass This Way Again," giving obvious pleasure to the congregation.

Our youth basketball team is back in action Wednesday at 8 PM in the recreation hall. Come out and watch us murder Christ the King.

Ladies, don't forget the rummage sale. It's a chance to get rid of those things not worth keeping around the house. Bring your husbands.

The Fasting and Prayer Conference includes meals.

Next Thursday, there will be tryouts for the choir. They need all the help they can get.

Potluck supper, Sunday at 5:00 PM, prayer and medication to follow.

Weight Watchers will meet at 7 PM at the First Presbyterian Church. Please use large double door at the side entrance.

The Low Self-Esteem Group will meet Thursday at 7:00 PM. Please use the back door.

The associate minister unveiled the church's new tithing campaign slogan last Sunday: "I Upped My Pledge. Up Yours."

REAL HEADLINES FROM REAL NEWSPAPERS

New Study of Obesity Looks for Larger Test Group

Astronaut Takes Blame for Gas in Spacecraft

Ban on Soliciting Dead in Trotwood

Enraged Cow Injures Farmer with Ax

Cold Wave Linked to Temperatures

Miners Refuse to Work after Death

Iraqi Head Seeks Arms

Include Your Children when Baking Cookies

Sisters Reunited after 18 Years at Checkout Counter

Family Lost in Corn Maze Calls 911

Juvenile Court to Try Shooting Defendant

Plane Too Close to Ground, Crash Probe Told

On a hairdryer: Do not use while sleeping.

Posted on a farm gate: KEEP OUT. Guard dog is loose. Survivors will be prosecuted.

Sign posted in a gas station: COURTEOUS AND EFFICIENT SELF-SERVICE

Sign in a store window: We buy old furniture. We sell antiques.

In a pawnshop window: See us at your earliest inconvenience.

Misprint in a newspaper: The driver approached the coroner at 90 miles per hour.

On the wall of a psychiatrist's office: No one in their right mind ever comes to see me.

On a child's superhero costume: Wearing of this garment does not enable you to fly.

On a bar of Dial soap: Directions: use like regular soap.

On a bag of chips: You could be a winner! No purchase necessary. Details inside.

On the box with a shower cap found in a hotel bathroom: Fits one head

On a jar of peanuts: Warning! Contains nuts!

Printed on the bottom of a frozen dessert: Do not turn package upside down.

On a bottle of sleeping pills: Warning: may cause drowsiness.

On a bottle of children's cough medicine: Do not drive car or operate machinery.

On a blender from Japan: Not to be used for the other use.

On an airline packet of nuts: Directions: open packet, eat nuts.

On a string of Christmas lights made in China: For indoor or outdoor use only.

On a subway train: Ladies, the poles are fitted for your safety. NO DANCING!

On a septic cleaning truck: CAUTION. STOOLBUS.

And its license plate: POO PMPR

And stencilled on its side: CAUTION. VEHICLE MAY BE CARRYING POLITICAL PROMISES

On a machine: CAUTION. THIS MACHINE HAS NO BRAIN. USE YOUR OWN.

Scrawled in lipstick on a diner counter: We waited 30 min, NO SERVICE

In a bar's bathroom. PLEASE DON'T THROW YOUR CIGARETTE BUTTS ON THE FLOOR. THE COCKROACHES ARE GETTING CANCER.

On the door of a restaurant's one bathroom: Our aim is to keep this bathroom clean.
GENTLEMEN: your aim will help. Stand closer. It's shorter than you think.
LADIES: Please remain seated for the entire performance.

ATTENTION DOG WALKERS: PICK UP AFTER YOUR DOGS. THANK YOU.
ATTENTION, DOGS: GRRR, WOOF, BARK. GOOD DOG.

CREMATION? Think outside the box!

On a Korean kitchen knife: Warning! Keep out of children.

Posted on a wall: TODAY IS THE OLDEST YOU'VE EVER BEEN, YET THE YOUNGEST YOU'LL EVER BE, SO ENJOY THIS DAY WHILE IT LASTS!

On another wall: You can say a lot of bad things about pedophiles. But at least they always drive slowly past schools.

GOLDEN YEARS BUMPER STICKERS

I'm in the initial stages of my golden years: SS, CD's, IRA's, AARP...

I asked my wife if old men wear boxers or briefs?

She said Depends.

I'm so old, I no longer buy green bananas

That Snap Crackle Pop in the morning...ain't my bowl of Rice Krispies.

The secret of staying young is to live honestly ... eat slowly ... and lie about your age.

FLORIDA: God's waiting room

I'm getting so old, that whenever I eat out, they ask me for my money up front.

I'm not old ... I'm Chronologically Gifted!

We got married for better or worse. He couldn't do better and I couldn't do worse.

I was always taught to respect my elders. Now I don't have anyone to respect.

On a bumper: I Brake for No Apparent Reaso

Bumper sticker: a closed mouth gathers no feet.

PLEASE BE SAFE.
Do not stand, sit, climb or lean on zoo fences.
If you fall, animals could eat you and that might make them sick.
Thank you.

In the window of Stein's jewelry store: Mr. Stein has had an expensive divorce and now needs the money, so come in, SALE ON NOW!

We'll be friends until we are old and senile. Then, we'll be NEW friends.

Taped to a men's room wall: If you sometimes feel a llttle useless, offended or depressed...always remember than you were once the fastest and most victorious little sperm out of millions.

Pasted on a building wall: DON'T HIT KIDS. No, seriously. They have guns now.

On the men's room wall in a bar:
One day long, long ago, there lived a woman who did not whine, nag or bitch.

But it was a long time ago, and it was just that one day.

On a bumper: I is a college student

Posted in a conference room: When trouble arises, there is always one individual who perceives a solution and is willing to command.

Very often, that person is crazy.

Tacked to a tree: PRIVATE SIGN. DO NOT READ.

Store in a small town: FAMILY JEWELS

WE WILL NO LONGER ACCEPT MONEY OUT OF UNDERGARMENTS

On a department store bulletin board: PLEASE NOTE. As of October 27th all staff will be required to report for work with teeth. If you don't have, please provide proof that you are getting some.

Hand-drawn sign above road work cones: YOU'LL NEVER GET TO WORK ON TIME HAHAHA!!

Posted on a parking lot fence: ATTENTION! Do not leave items of value in vehicle. You are in Middletown, not Fairyland.

At the entrance to Kosi Bay Bush Camp: WARNING! Fasten brastraps and remove dentures. VERY BUMPY ROAD.

On a busy road: SLOW DOWN! THE COP HIDES BEHIND THIS SIGN!

SAVE ENERGY! How would you like it if someone turned you on and then left?

Road sign: SLOW DOWN or DIE

At the side of a suburban road:
PLEASE DRIVE SLOWLY...and watch for
OLD HORSES
BLIND DOGS
UNRULY KIDS
for the next two miles

POO PING THAI CHINESE CUISINE

On Route 1: DELUXE MOTEL
HIGHLY RECOMMENDED BY OWNER

On a country road: Seeking a sign from God?
THIS IS IT!

AUCTION
SUNDAY, NOV. 1, 3:00 PM
NEW AND USED
FOOD

SAMSON'S EAT HERE AND GET GAS

Highway sign: I GOT MY CRABS FROM DIRTY DICK'S CRAB SHACK

PETS NEW AND USED

In a movie theater: Anyone caught EXITING thru this door will be asked to LEAVE!

In front of a church:
DON'T LET WORRIES KILL YOU
LET THE CHURCH HELP

GIVE BLOOD. 8 billion mosquitos can't be wrong.

Above a urinal: THIS WATER IS NOT FOR DRINKING

At the side of a road: CAUTION! THIS SIGN HAS SHARP EDGES. Do not touch the edges of this sign!

In a men's room: Please refrain from standing on the toilet bowl as an accident is going to happen.

On a restaurant's double doors:
Left side: PLEASE USE OTHER DOOR
Right side: THIS ONE IS THE OTHER DOOR

Diamond sign on road: CAUTION...WATER ON ROAD DURING RAIN

PONDEROSA VETERINARY HOSPITAL: SPAY OR NEUTER YOUR BEST FRIEND

Death is nature's way of saying, Slow Down

BUMPER STICKERS WE HAVE DRIVEN BEHIND

My Karma ran over your Dogma

If you can read this, I can hit my brakes and sue you!

I brake for ... AAAAGHHH!!! ... NO BRAKES!

Ask me about my vow of silence.

I killed a 6-pack just to watch it die.

MY CHILD WAS Trustee of the Month at ALCATRAZ

Few women admit their age. Few men act it.

I don't suffer from insanity; I enjoy every minute of it.

This is NOT an abandoned vehicle

Born Free ... Taxed to Death

Work is for people who don't know how to fish

Cover me...I'm changing lanes.

Auntie Em. Hate you. Hate Kansas. Taking the dog. Dorothy

Earn cash in your spare time. Blackmail your friends.

A penny saved is ridiculous.

Hang up and drive!

AMBIVALENT? Well... yes and no

I'm not tense, just terribly, terribly alert.

Is it time for your medication or mine?

Don't bother me, I'm living happily ever after.

Better living through denial.

Chaos, Panic, Disorder! My work here is done!

It's lonely at the top, but you eat better.

WANTED: Meaningful overnight relationship

If you are psychic, think "HONK!"

Forget world peace. Visualize using your turn signal.

Grow your own dope. Plant a man.

I want it all and I want it delivered.

My dog can lick anyone!

Rehab is for quitters!

On a tshirt: Never Underestimate the Power of Stupid People in Large Groups

On a baby's shirt: Party ... My Crib ... 2 AM

MONTANA GRIZZLY BEAR NOTICE
We advise that outdoorsmen wear noisy little bells on their clothing to warn bears of their presence.
We also advise outdoorsmen to carry pepper spray in case of an encounter with a bear.
It is also a good idea to watch out for fresh signs of bear activity. Outdoorsmen should recognize the difference between black bear dung and grizzly bear dung.
Black bear dung is smaller and contains lots of berries and squirrel fur. Grizzly bear dung has little bells in it and smells like pepper.

On a woman's t-shirt: I'm not 50–I'm 18 with 32 years of experience

On another woman's t-shirt: I'm not getting older. I'm getting meaner.

Bumper sticker: That was Zen. This is Tao.

On a tshirt: DISREGARD LAST T-SHIRT.

On a man's t-shirt: I'm retired and this is as dressed up as I'm gonna get.

Another one: I Do Whatever the Voices Tell Me to Do

Yet another: Parents of Teenagers know why animals eat their young.

On a tshirt: I'm done! D-U-N!

House sign: BEWARE OF ... WELL, JUST BEWARE

Road sign: Boring Oregon City - Exit 1 mi.

Roadside sign: PLEASE DON'T EMPTY YOUR DOG HERE!

Best no-parking sign ever:
DO NOT PARK HERE
The wrath of the ancients will fall upon your head. Your shoelaces will not stay tied. Rabid squirrels will invade your home. Food in your refrigerator will mysteriously spoil. Your vehicle will start making that expensive knocking sound again. And NO-ONE WILL TALK TO YOU AT PARTIES.
You will also seriously piss off the woman who pays good money for this garage space and believe me, you don't want that.

SILLY QUESTIONS

SILLY QUESTIONS

Why is it called "after dark" when it's really after light?

Why do tug boats actually push their barges?

If a word were misspelled in a dictionary, how would we ever know?

Isn't it strange that the third hand on a watch is known as the second hand?

Why do we say that something is "out of whack?" What's a whack?

Why do "slow up" and "slow down" mean the same thing?

If all the world's a stage, where is the audience sitting?

If love is blind, why is lingerie so popular?

Why is bra singular and panties plural?

What's the similarity between a tornado and an Alabama divorce?
Somebody's gonna lose a trailer.

What should a woman say to a man she's just had sex with?
Anything she wants. He's asleep.

What's the fastest way to a man's heart?
Through his chest with a sharp knife.

Why didn't Noah swat those two mosquitoes?

Why do they sterilize the needle for lethal injections?

If flying is so safe, why do they call the airport the terminal?

What do you call a handcuffed man?
Trustworthy.

What does it mean when a man is in your bed gasping for breath and calling your name?
You didn't hold the pillow down long enough.

What's the difference between in-laws and outlaws? Outlaws are wanted.

What's the source of virgin wool?
Ugly sheep.

What man has married many women, yet stays a bachelor?
A priest.

What is it you can keep, even after giving it?
Your word.

What gets wet while drying?
A towel.

What comes once in a minute, twice in a moment, and never in a thousand years?
The letter M.

The more you take, the more you leave behind. What are they?
Your footsteps.

What belongs solely to you, which others use much more than you do?
Your name.

What is it that you will break as soon as you name it?
Silence.

What is put on a table, cut, but never eaten?
A deck of cards.

What is it that the more you take away, the bigger it becomes?
A hole.

It's been around for millions of years, yet is only a month old.
The moon.

How do you get $63 in bills, without using any $1 bills or any coins?

One $50 bill ...One $5 bill . . .Four $2 bills

Forward I am heavy, backward I am not. What am I?
A ton.

What's special about the following sequence of numbers: 8 5 4 9 1 7 6 10 3 2 0?
They're in alphabetical order.

You are the driver of a city bus. 28 passengers get on at the first stop. At the second stop, 12 of them get off, and 6 more get on. At the third stop, 8 get off and 2 get on. At the fourth stop, 4 get off and 10 get on. At the last stop, all get off. What color are the driver's eyes?

What color are yours? You're the driver.

If an egg came floating down the Hudson River to New York City, where did it come from?
A chicken.

How many times can you subtract the number 5 from the number 25?
Once. After that, the number is no longer 25.

What can run but never walks, has a mouth but never talks, has a head but never weeps, has a bed but never sleeps?
A river.

I have holes in my top and in my bottom, and all over. Yet, I hold water. What am I?
A sponge.

Arnold Schwarzenegger has a big one.
Michael J. Fox has a small one.
Madonna doesn't have one.
The Pope has one but doesn't use it.
Clinton uses his all the time.
Bush is one.
Jerry Seinfeld is very proud of his.
Cher claims she took on three.
They never saw Lucy use Desi's.
What is it?
Don't look at the answer right away.
The answer is: A last name.
(If you thought anything else, shame on you.)

Ever wonder about those people who spend $3.00 a bottle for Evian water?

Try spelling Evian backwards.

Isn't making a smoking section in a restaurant like making a peeing section in a swimming pool?

Why isn't the number 11 pronounced onety-one?

What hair color do they put on the drivers' licenses of bald men?

If it's true that we're here to help others, then what are the others here for?

Why do they put pictures of criminals in Post Offices? Are we supposed to write to them? Why don't they just put their photographs on postage stamps and then the mail people can look for them while they deliver the mail?

Why do drugstores make the sick walk all the way to the back of the store to get their medications, while healthy people can buy candy and cigarettes at the front?

Why do we leave our cars, worth thousands of dollars, in the driveway; and fill the garage with useless junk?

Why do they sell hot dogs in packages of six; and hot dog buns in packages of eight?

Why does the sun lighten our hair but darken our skin?

Why can't women apply mascara with their mouth closed?

Why is the time of day with the slowest traffic called Rush Hour?

You know that black box that's always intact after a plane crash? Why don't they make the entire place out of that stuff?

What can a man do while his wife is going through menopause? Keep busy. If you're handy with tools, build a room in the basement. Then you'll have a place to live when you are finished.

A crook is condemned to death. He has to choose between three doors. Behind the first there are raging fires. The second is full of men with loaded guns and the third is full of lions that haven't eaten in three years. Which room is safest?
The third room, of course. Lions that haven't eaten for three years are all dead.

What often falls but never gets hurt? Rain.

Can you name three consecutive days without using the words Wednesday, Friday, or Sunday?

Sure you can. Today, yesterday, and tomorrow.

What is odd about this unusual paragraph? I'm curious as to just how quickly you can find out what is so unusual about it. It looks so ordinary and plain and that you would think nothing was wrong with it. In fact, nothing is wrong with it! It is highly unusual, though. Study it and think about it; but you still may not find anything odd. But if you work at it a bit, you might find out. Try to do it without any coaching. Okay. The answer is that the letter "e", the most common letter in the English language, does not appear at all in it.

How does a slight tax increase cost you $200 and a substantial tax cut saves you $30?

Have you ever thought of taking a lesson from the weather? It pays no attention to criticism.

What is Globalization? Princess Diana's death. Because an English Princess with an Egyptian boyfriend crashes in a French tunnel while riding in a German car with a Dutch engine driven by a Gelgian who was drunk on Scottish whisky, followed closely by Italian paparazzi on Japanese motorcycles and treated by an American doctor.

Whoever said that condoms are completely safe? A friend of mine was wearing one and got hit by a bus.

What do you get when a naked man ties a string around his waist with a potato dangling at the end? A dick tater.

Sex may be overrated, but can you imagine where everything else stands?

Are you free tonight, or will it cost me?

What is a zebra? 26 sizes up from an "A" bra.

What's the definition of macho? Jogging home from your own vastectomy.

How do you get four old ladies to shout a dirty word? Get a fifth old lady to shout "Bingo!"

What happens if you kiss a canary? You get chirpes, it can't be tweeted because it's a canarial disease.

What's the difference between men and government bonds? Bonds mature.

What's the difference between sex for money and sex for love? Sex for money costs a lot less.

What should you do if you find your ex-husband rolling around on the ground in agony? Shoot him again.

What do you call the useless piece of skin on the end of a man's penis? His body.

Why do female black widow spiders kill their males right after mating?
It stops the snoring before it starts.

What the best way to kill a man?
Put a naked woman and a six-pack in front o him. Then tell him he can pick only one.

Why do doctors smack babies on their butts right after birth?
To knock the penises off the smart ones.

How does a man keep his youth?
By giving her money, furs, and diamonds.

How do you keep your husband from reading your email?
ename your mail folder "instruction manual."

What's the difference between men and women?
She wants one man to satisfy her every need. He wants many women to satisfy his one need.

If women are so darn perfect at multitasking, how come they can't have a headache and sex at the same time?

Why do Scotsmen wear kilts? Because it's easier to run with your kilt up than with your pants down.

Why don't satanic warlocks ever go on television to exhort unbelievers to donate money to fight God?

If you throw a red stone into a blue sea, what will it become?
Wet.

How can a man go eight days without sleep?
He sleeps at night.

Approximately how many birthdays does the average Chinese woman have? One. The rest are all anniversaries.

What is it that no person ever saw which never was but always will be?
Tomorrow.

Why couldn't the pirate play cards? Because he was sitting on the deck.

Why do birds fly South every Fall?
Because it's too far to walk.

What is it that shakes and twitches and can be found on the ocean bottom?
A nervous wreck.

What lettuce was served at the salad bar on the Titanic?
Iceberg.

Why are there so many people named Smith in the phonebook?
Because they have phones.

On a turkey, which side would you find feathers?
On the outside.

Where would you find a dog with one leg?
Exactly where you left it.

Why did the room packed with married people seem empty?
Not a single person was there.

How do you know you are flying on a "no frills" airline?
You need exact change to board.

What did the cowboy say when he went into the car dealership in Germany?
Audi.

What gets wet with drying?
A towel.

Bay of Bengal is in what state?
Liquid.

Why is it easy to weigh a fish?
Because it has its own scales.

What kind of bow can never be tied?
Rainbow.

Why do traffic lights rarely go swimming?
They take much too long to change.

What would you have if you crossed a cheetah with a beef burger?
Really fast food.

Why did Tim take a prune out for the evening?
He couldn't get a date.

What is another name for female Viagra? A diamond.

What looks like half an apple? The other half.

How do people in prison talk to each other? Cell phones.

How many animals can you fit into a pair of pantyhose? Now think about it. Ready?

10 little piggies
2 calves
1 ass

And an unknown number of hares.

RETIREMENT Q & A

Q: How many days in a week?
A: 6 Saturdays, 1 Sunday.

Q: When is a retiree's bedtime?
A: Three hours after he falls asleep on the couch.

Q: What's a retired person's biggest gripe?
A: There's not enough time to get everything done.

Q: Why don't retired people mind being called Senior Citizens?
A: The term comes with a 10% discount.

Q: Among retired folks, what is considered formal attire?
A: Tied shoes.

Q: Why do retired people count pennies?
A: They're the only ones who have the time.

What do you call a man who was born in Atlanta, lived in Los Angeles, and died in New York?
Dead.

What would you call a girl who has three boyfriends named William? A Bill collector.

What do you do if your spouse walks out? You shut the door.

The children of Israel wandered in the desert for 40 years. What does this show us?
Even in Biblical times, men wouldn't ask for directions.

Wouldn't it be nice if you could go to the movies and see a picture as good as the coming attractions look?

How did the fool and his money get together in the first place?

Wouldn't it be a lot simpler to isolate and label the few things that aren't harmful to your health?

Isn't it hard to believe that this nation was founded partly to avoid taxes?

If practice makes perfect and nobody's perfect... why practice?

How do I set my laser printer to stun?

In a country of free speech, why are there telephone bills?

How many roads must a man travel down before he admits he is lost?

If you had everything, where would you put it?

Why does a slight tax increase cost you two hundred dollars and a substantial tax cut save you thirty cents?

How is it that one careless match can start a forest fire, but it takes a whole box to start a campfire?

Why does a man's heart beat faster when a woman wears a leather dress?

It's because she smells like a new truck!

What is it that even the most careful person overlooks? His nose.

What if the Hokey Pokey is what it's all about?

If two's company and three's a crowd, what are four and five? Nine.

What do you call an American drawing? Yankee Doodle.

What do you call a train loaded with toffee? A chew chew train.

What do you call a country where everyone drives a red car? A red carnation.

How was the Roman Empire cut in half? With a pair of Caesars!

Why don't penguins fly? They're not tall enough to be pilots.

How do you tell the difference between a cow and a bull?

Try milking them both. The one that smiles is the bull.

What was the best thing before they sold sliced bread?

How do you know when it's time to tune your bagpipes?

Why aren't there any B batteries?

If the pen is mightier than the sword and a picture is worth a thousand words, how dangerous is a fax?

In a country of free speech, why do we have telephone bills?

Isn't it strange that a building burns down at the same time it burns up?

How does skating on thin ice get you into hot water?

If the shortest distance between two points is a straight line, then why does it take so long when you're standing in one?

If someone has a mid-life crisis while playing hide and seek, does he automatically lose because he can't find himself?

Should crematoriums give discounts to burn victims?

What do you get when you cross a dog with a telephone?

A golden receiver.

If you put THE and IRS together doesn't it become THEIRS?

How do we know that the Earth won't come to an end?

Because it's round.

REMEMBER KNOCK-KNOCK JOKES?
Knock knock
Who's there?
Button. Button who?
Button in is not polite!

Knock knock
Who's there?
Candy. Candy who?
Candy cow jump over de moon?

Knock knock
Who's there?
Ice cream soda. Ice cream soda who?
Ice cream soda whole world will know what a nut you are!

Knock knock
Who's there?
Scissor. Scissor who?
Scissor and Cleopatra!

Knock knock
Who's there?
Scold. Scold who?
Scold outside!

Knock knock
Who's there?
Scott. Scott who?
Scott to be me 'cause it ain't you!

Knock knock
Who's there?
Little old lady. Little old lady who?
I didn't know you could yodel!

Knock knock
Who's there?
Turnip. Turnip who?
Turnip the heat, it's cold in here!

Knock knock
Who's there?
Twig. Twig who?
Twig or tweat!

Knock knock
Who's there?
Livia. Livia who?
Livia me along!

Knock knock
Who's there?
Liszt. Liszt who?
Liszt of ingredients!

Knock knock
Who's there?
Lisa. Lisa who?
Lisa you could do is let me in!

Why do birds fly South in the winter? Because it's too far to walk.

What is out of bounds? An exhausted kangeroo.

Have you ever seen a duchess? Yes, it's the same as an English "s."

What followed the dinosaur? It's tail.

Would you like a duck egg for breakfast? Only if you quack it for me.

Did you hear about the mad scientist who put dynamite in the fridge? They say it blew his cool.

I've got a wonder watch that cost only fifty cents.

Why is it a wonder watch?

Because every time I took at it, I wonder if it's still working.

How long did the Hundred Year War last? 116 years, from 1337 to 1453.

What was King George VI's first name? Albert.

What country makes Panama hats? Ecuador.

What if there were no hypothetical questions?

Would a fly without wings be called a walk?

If you spin an Asian man in a circle three times, does he become disoriented?

If one synchronized swimmer drowns, do the rest of them drown, too?

If a turtle doesn't have a shell, is he homeless or naked?

If you ate pasta and antipasto, would you still be hungry?

What disease did cured ham have?

Why are actors IN movies but ON television?

If a deaf person goes to court, do they still call it a hearing?

If nobody cares that Jimmy cracked corn, then why are we still singing about it?

Why do toasters always have a setting that burns the toast?

Can you cry underwater?

Who decided that a round pizza should go in a square box?

Why do we say we slept like a baby when babies wake up every two hours?

How come we put a man on the moon before we realized it would be a good idea to put luggage on wheels?

We say, "It's Greek to me." What do Greeks say? (Answer: "It's Chinese to me.")

Can you use the car-pool lane if you're driving a hearse with a corpse in the back?

How is a healthy person like the United States?

They both have good constitutions.

What quacks, has webbed feet, and betrays his country?

Beneduck Arnold

What kind of tea did the American colonists thirst for?

Liberty!

What dog protest occurred in 1773?

The Boston Flea Party

What ghost haunted King George III?

The Spirit of '76!

Why did Paul Revere ride his horse from Boston to Lexington?

Because the horse was too heavy to carry.

How can a woman speed up the heart rate of her 65-year-old husband?

Tell him she's pregnant.

Where can a man in his 70s find a younger, pretty woman who is interested in him?

Try the bookstore under fiction.

What is the most common remark made by retirees in an antique shop?

I remember that.

Why should older folks use valet parking?

The valet won't forget where the car's parked.

Is it common for older men and women to have trouble with memory storage?
Not at all. The problem is with retrieval.

What would you get if you crossed a patriot with a small curly-haired dog?
Yankee Poodle.

Did you hear the one about the Liberty Bell?
Yeah, it cracked me up.

Do people sleep more soundly as they age?
Yes, but usually in the afternoon.

Why are teddy bears never hungry?
They're stuffed.

What did the judge say when the skunk came into the courtroom?
Odor in the court!

What sound do porcupines make when they make love? OUCH!

What did the buffalo say to his child when he went away on a trip? Bison.

What is "out of bounds?"
An exhausted kangeroo.

What animals live on documents?
Seals!

What did one flea say to another?
Shall we walk or take a dog?

Why do fish live in salt water?
Because pepper makes them sneeze.

What march would you play at a jungle parade?
'Tarzan Stripes Forever"

What did one flag say to the other flag?
Nothing. It just waved.

What dance was very popular in 1776?
Indepen-dance.

What was the craziest battle of the American Revolution?
The Battle of Bonkers Hill.

What do you call a good looking, intelligent, sensitive man?
A rumor.

Why do little boys whine?
They're practicing to be men.

What do you call a handcuffed man?
Trustworthy.

What does it mean when a man is in your bed gasping for breath and calling your name?
You didn't hold the pillow down long enough.

Why do female black widwo spiders kill their males after mating?
To stop the snoring before it starts.

I was asked: One thing that is commonly found in cells. Apparently "Mexicans" is not the correct answer.

Can you order a bomber jacket from a Muslim clothing store?

What do you call a man without arms or legs, who's in a pile of leaves? Russell.

What do you call a man without arms or legs, hanging on the wall? Art.

What do you do with a man who makes faces all day? A clockmaker.

What do you give a 900-pound gorilla for his birthday?
I don't know, but he'd better like it!

What do you call a bee that's always complaining? A grumble bee.

What do you call a cat that plays football? Puss in Boots.

How much does it cost for a pirate to have his ears pierced? A buck an ear. Arghhhh!

What do you call cheese that doesn't belong to you? Nacho cheese.

What do you call someone who doesn't have all their fingers on one hand?

Normal. You have fingers on both hands.

What do you call four bullfighters in quicksand? Quattro sinko.

Do you realize that some tax forms ask you to check a box if you are BLIND?

Who audits IRS agents?

What happens when you cross a snowman with a vampire? Frostbite.

How do you know that a blonde has been using your computer? There's white-out on the screen.

WITTY OBSERVATIONS

WITTY OBSERVATIONS

Always keep your words soft and sweet, in case you have to eat them.

If you can't be kind, at least have the decency to be vague.

Never put both feet in your mouth at the same time because then you won't have a leg to stand on.

When everything's coming your way, you're in the wrong lane.

Birthdays are good for you. The more you have, the longer you live.

Drive carefully. It's not only cars that can be recalled by their maker.

The early bird still has to eat worms.

Some mistakes are too much fun to make only once.

I joined a health club last year. Cost me over $500 and I haven't lost a pound. Apparently, you have to go there.

We all get heavier as we get older because there's a lot more information in our heads. That's my story and I'm sticking to it.

Exercise can add years to your life. This enables you, at 85 years, to spend an additional five months in a nursing home at $7,000 a month.

Do they hold elections in November because it's the best time for picking a turkey?

I asked my mother if I was a gifted child...she said they certainly wouldn't have paid for me.

You spend the first two years of your childrens' lives teaching them to walk and talk. Then you spend the next sixteen telling them to sit down and shut up.

I won't say that my bank gives terrible service, but today when I asked the teller to check my balance, she leaned over and pushed me.

Don't think of it as hot flashes. Think of it as your inner child playing with matches.

98% of Americans say, "Oh damn!" as the car slides into the ditch on a slippery road. The other 2% are from Texas and they say, "Hold my beer and watch this!"

I'm against picketing, but I'm not sure how to show it.

I've still got it but nobody wants to see it.

A little boy asked his mother where his intelligence came from. "You must have gotten it from your father," she said, "because I still have mine."

A man asks a wizard if he can remove a curse he's been living with for forty years.

"Perhaps," says the wizard. "But I will need to know the exact word used to put the curse on you."

"I now pronounce you man and wife."

A little girl was diligently pounding on the keyboard of her grandfather's computer. "What are you writing?" he asked. "I don't know," she replied. "I can't read yet."

When you feel blue and think you would like to go back to your youth, think of Algebra.

SPECIAL OBSERVATIONS OF STEVEN WRIGHT:

99% of the lawyers give the rest a bad name.

Depression is merely anger without enthusiasm.

How do you tell when you're out of invisible ink?

All those who believe in psychokinesis, raise my hand.

If everything seems to be going well, you have obviously overlooked something.

A clear conscience is usually the sign of a bad memory.

I intend to live forever ... so far, so good.

The sooner you fall behind, the more time you'll have to catch up.

Experience is something you don't get until just after you need it.

If at first you don't succeed, destroy all evidence that you tried.

WHAT PAPER DO YOU READ?

The Wall Street Journal is read by people who run the country.

The Washington Post is read by people who think they run the country.

The New York Times is read by people who think they should be running the country.

The Boston Globe is read by people whose parents used to run the country and they did a far superior job of it, thank you very much.

The NY Daily News is read by people who don't care who's running the country, and don't really care as long as they can get a seat on the subway.

The San Francisco Chronicle is read by people who aren't sure there is a country or that anyone is running it; but whomever it is, they oppose all that they stand for.

The Miami Herald is read by people who are running another country, but need the baseball scores.

The National Enquirer is read by people trapped in line at the supermarket.

The nice thing about being senile is you can hide your own Easter eggs.

I believe in sharing the road with other drivers. They can have the part behind me.

Married men live longer than single men; but married men are a lot more willing to die.

A woman marries a man expecting he will change, but he doesn't.
A man marries a woman expecting that she won't change, and she does.

A woman has the last word in any argument. Anything a man says after that is the beginning of a new argument.

My wife Mary and I have been married for 47 years and not once have we had an argument serious enough to consider divorce. Murder, yes, but divorce, never. –Jack Benny

The reason Congressmen try so hard to get re-elected is that they would hate to have to make a living under the laws they've passed.

Women and cats will do as they please. Men and dogs should relax and get used to the idea.

GEORGE CARLIN GEMS

As a matter of principle, I never attend the first annual anything.

Frisbeetarianism is the belief that when you die, your soul goes up on the roof and gets stuck.

I'm not concerned with all hell breaking loose; but that a PART of hell will break loose...it'll be much harder to detect.

Some national parks have long waiting lists for camping reservations. When you have to wait a year to sleep next to a tree, something is wrong.

There's no present. There's only the immediate future and the recent past.

Think of how stupid the average person is, and realize that half of them are stupider than that.

If lawyers are disbarred and clergymen defrocked, doesn't it follow that electricians can be delighted and musicians denoted?

Weather forecast for tonight: dark. Continued dark overnight, with widely scattered light by morning.

Here's a little-known fact: the first testicular guard "cup" was used in hockey in 1874 and the first helmet was used in 1974.

That means it took 100 years for men to realize that their brain is also important.

I saw a woman wearing a sweatshirt with "Guess" on it. So I said, "Implants?" She hit me.

How come we choose from just two people to run for President, and over fifty for Miss America?

Don't argue with an idiot. People watching may not be able to tell the difference.

Bad news: Brain cells come and brain cells go; but fat cells live forever.

I was so depressed last night thinking about the economy, wars, jobs, Social Security, retirement funds, and everything, that I called the Suicide Lifeline.

I was forwarded to a call center in Pakistan and when I told them I was suicidal, they asked if I could drive a truck.

A good friend will come and bail you out of jail; but a true friend will be sitting next to you, saying, "Wow, that was fun!"

It takes one million sperm to fertilize one egg. You know why? They won't stop and ask for directions.

Definition of a teenager: God's punishment for enjoying sex.

Today is the oldest you've ever been, yet the youngest you'll ever be. So enjoy this day while it lasts.

It's not what you gather, but what you scatter that tells what kind of life you have lived.

When a man steals your wife, there is no better revenge than to let him keep her.

War does not determine who is right... only who is left.

A clear conscience is the sign of a fuzzy memory.

When tempted to fight fire with fire, remember: the Fire Department usually uses water.

Always keep several get well cards on the mantle, so if unexpected guests arrive, they'll think you've been sick and unable to clean.

WHAT I LEARNED FROM MY MOTHER

My mother taught me how to become an adult: "If you don't eat your vegetables, you'll never grow up."

My mother taught me wisdom: "When you get to be my age, you'll understand."

My mother taught me ESP: "Put on a sweater. You're cold."

My mother taught me medical science: "If you keep crossing your eyes, they'll freeze that way."

My mother taught me about religion: "You'd better pray that comes out of the carpet!"

My mother taught me logic: "Because I said so, that's why."

My mother taught me irony: "Keep crying and I'll give you something to *really* cry about!"

My mother taught me genetics: "You're just like your father."

And about justice: "When you grow up and have kids, I hope you have one just like you!"

Never buy a car you can't push.

Always read stuff that will make you look intelligent if you die in the middle of it.

Since it's the early worm that gets eaten by the bird ... sleep late!

A truly happy person is one who can enjoy the scenery on a detour.

Save the Earth. It's the only planet with chocolate!

Marriage is a relationship in which one person is always right, and the other is usually the husband.

Aging: first you forget names, then you forget faces. Then you forget to pull up your zipper.

It's worse when you forget to pull it down.

Some people try to turn back their personal odometers. Not me! I want people to know why I look this way. I've traveled a long distance and some of the roads weren't paved.

Maybe this world is some other planet's Hell.

FROM THE LIPS OF GEORGE CARLIN

Honesty may be the best policy but it's important to remember that, apparently, by elimination, dishonesty is the second-best policy.

As soon as someone is identified as an unsung hero, he no longer is.

I don't have hobbies; hobbies cost money. Interests, on the other hand, are quite free.

If it requires a uniform, it's a useless endeavor.

Just when I discovered the meaning of life, they changed it.

No one knows what's next, but everybody does it.

You can't fight City Hall, but you can sure blow it up.

A house is just a place to keep your stuff while you go out and get more stuff.

I'm not into working out. My philosophy is no pain, no pain.

HARD TIMES

My neighbor got a pre-declined credit card in the mail.

I saw a Mormon with only one wife.

CEO's are now playing miniature golf.

If the bank returns a check marked "insufficient funds," call and ask them if they meant you or them.

A picture is now worth only 210 words.

Parents in Beverly Hills fired teir nannies and learned their children's names.

I was so depressed by the economy, wars, and retirement funds, I called the Suicide Hotline. I reached a call center in Pakistan and when I told them I was suicidal, they got all excited and asked if I could drive a truck.

A truckload of Americans was caught trying to sneak into Mexico.

My cousin had an exorcism but couldn't pay for it, so they repossessed her.

CAN'T GET ENOUGH OF GEORGE CARLIN

By and large, language is a tool for concealing the truth.

Death is caused by swallowing small amounts of saliva over a long period of time.

Future historians will be able to study at the Jimmy Carter Library, the Gerald Ford Library, the Ronald Reagan Library, and the Bill Clinton Adult Bookstore.

I'm in shape. Round is a shape.

In comic strips, the person on the right always speaks first.

Inside every cynical person, there is a disappointed idealist.

May the forces of evil become confused on the way to your house.

One tequila, two tequila, three tequila, floor.

Eventually, you will reach a point in your life when you stop lying about your age and start bragging about it.

The older we get, the fewer things seem worth waiting in line for.

Long ago, when men cursed and beat the ground with sticks, it was called witchcraft.

Today, we know it as golf.

If you don't learn to laugh at trouble, you won't have anything to laugh at when you're old.

The cardiologist's diet: if it tastes good, spit it out.

Short summary of every major Jewish holiday: They tried to destroy us. We won. Let's eat.

Our bombs are smarter than the average high school student. At least they can find Kuwait.

Always go to other peoples' funerals; otherwise, they won't come to yours. -Yogi Berra

Contrary to popular belief, "Damn It" is not God's last name.

The best cure for insomnia is to get a lot of sleep. -W. C. Fields

If two wrongs don't make a right, try three.

If we don't succeed, we run the risk of failure. -Dan Quayle.

As long as people will accept crap, it will be financially profitable to dispense it. -Dick Cavett

Why do they call it rush hour when nothing moves?

If I were two-faced, would I be wearing this one? -Abraham Lincoln

2/3 of American can't do fractions. The other ½ just don't care.

Everyone has a right to be stupid. Some just abuse the privilege.

Crime doesn't pay. Does that mean my job is a crime?

Smoking is one of the major causes of statistics.

If your parents never had children, chances are you won't either. -Dick Cavett

Eat well. Stay fit. Die anyway.

Don't judge a book by its movie.

The next time you think you're perfect, try walking on water.

I tried switching to gum, but I couldn't keep it lit.

Marriage is one of the chief causes of divorce.

A wise man washes his hands after he pees. A wiser man doesn't pee on his hands.

Today is the tomorrow we worried about yesterday.

People who think they know everything are a great annoyance to those of us who do.

What happens if you get scared half to death, twice?

The guy who invented the wheel was okay. But the guy who invented the other three... he was the real genius!

When you're run down, the best thing to take is the license number.

Statistics show that every two minutes another statistic is created.

When you come to a fork in the road... take it. -Yogi Berra

It is generally agreed that 'hello" is an appropriate greeting because if you came into a room and said "goodbye," it could confuse a lot of people.

If everything seems to be going well, you have obviously overlooked something. -S. Wright

Men are like parking spots. All the good ones are taken and the rest are handicapped.

Men are like lava lamps. Fun to look at, but not very bright.

Education will never become as expensive as ignorance.

Life is pretty tough; but just think how much harder it would be if you couldn't sleep a third of it away.

If you have a good temper, keep it. If you have a bad temper, don't lose it.

FAMOUS LAST WORDS:

"I have traveled the length and breadth of this country and talked with the best people, and I can assure you that data processing is a fad that won't last out the year."

–editor of business books, 1967

"I think there is a world market for maybe five computers."

-Thos. Watson, chairman of IBM, 1943

"Computers in the future may weigh no more than 1.5 tons."

-Popular Mechanics, 1949

"There is no likelihood man can ever tap the power of the atom."

-Robt. Millikan, Nobel Prize in Physics, 1923

"The bomb will never go off. I speak as an expert in explosives."

-Adm. Wm. Leahy, US Atomic Bomb Project

"64K ought to be enough for anybody."

-Bill Gates, 1981

"Heavier-than-air machines are impossible."

–Lord Kelvin, President, Royal Society, 1895

"We don't like their sound, and guitar music is on the way out."

-Decca records, rejecting the Beatles, 1962

"Everything that can be invented, has been invented."

-Commissioner, US Office of Patents, 1899

"I'm just glad that it's Clark Gable who's falling on his face, and not Gary Cooper."

-Gary Cooper, on not taking the role of Rhett Butler in Gone with the Wind.

"Airplanes are interesting toys but of no military value."

-Marechal Ferdinand Foch, France, 1911

"The Americans have need of the telephone, but we do not. We have plenty of messenger boys."

–Sir Wm. Preece, British Post Office, 1876

"Who the hell wants to hear actors talk?"

-H. M. Warner, Warner Brothers, 1927

"With over 50 foreign cars already on sale here, the Japanese auto industry isn't likely to carve out a big slice of the U. S. market."

-Business Week, August 2, 1968

WILL ROGERS, COWBOY AND COMEDIAN, SAID:

Never slap a man who's chewing tobacco.

Never kick a cow-chip on a hot day.

There are two theories to arguing with a woman. Neither works.

Never miss a good chance to shut up.

Always drink upstream from the herd.

If you find yourself in a hole, stop digging.

There are three kinds of men: the ones who learn by reading. The few who learn by observation. The rest of them have to pee on the electric fence and find out for themselves.

If you're riding ahead of the herd, take a look back every now and then to make sure it's still there.

After eating an entire bull, a mountain lion felt so good he stated roaring. He kept it up until a hunter came along and shot him.

The moral: when you're full of bull, keep your mouth shut.

Faith will never die as long as full-color seed catalogs are printed.

If you keep your mouth shut, you'll get credit for knowing what you aren't talking about.

Just about the time a woman thinks her work is all done, she becomes a grandmother.

Some folks think that Mars can't support life. Well, it's not such an easy thing on Earth, either.

If we judged everything by appearance, nobody would ever eat a lobster.

There must have been some reason nature made man's ears to stay open and his mouth to shut.

Americans have more food to eat than anyone else in the world ... and more diets to keep them from eating it.

The large national debt our younger generation has inherited should keep them from one indulgence: ancestor worship.

The world seems to be full of people who speak twice before they think once.

George Washington set a bad example when he threw a dollar across the Potomac. They've been throwing money away in Washington ever since.

Women will never be equal to men until they can walk down the street with a bald spot and a pot belly and still think they're pretty amazing.

Immigration is the sincerest form of flattery.

Enjoy yourself today. These are the good old days you are to miss later on.

A lot of people drive like tomorrow isn't worth waiting for.

The first one to see a traffic light turn green is the second car in line.

The man who gives in when he is wrong is a wise man. The man who gives in when he is right is married.

Despite inflation, a penny for some people's thoughts is still a fair price.

Somehow, as we get older, work seems a lot less fun....and fun seems a lot more work.

If you're going to teach your children the value of a dollar, do it quick!

I can remember when it was cheaper to park the car than to drive it.

The world is full of willing people; some willing to work, the rest willing to let them. -Rob't Frost

Money isn't everything. Sometimes it's not even enough.

It's a good thing that beauty is only skin deep, or I'd be rotten to the core. -Phyllis Diller

Experience is a great teacher. A man never wakes his second baby to see it smile.

The secret of financial success is to spend what you have left after saving, instead of saving what you have left after spending.

For some reason, anger makes your mouth work faster than your mind.

This will never be a truly civilized country until we spend more money for books than for a pack of cigarettes.

With airlines today, you can experience the thrill of having breakfast in L.A., lunch in New York, dinner in London, and your luggage in Rome.

No one has ever been able to explain why a child cannot walk around a puddle.

Most advice can be had for nothing–and usually it's worth it.

The easiest thing in the world is to convince a person that she is overworked.

Most people can keep a secret. It's the folks they tell it to who cause the problem.

The worst thing about growing old is having to listen to a lot of advice from your children.

Too many of our highways seem to run on the theory that you don't need road manners if you're an SUV.

After you decide nothing can be done, someone comes along and does it.

The driver is safer when the roads are dry and the roads are safer when the driver is dry.

For bringing a family closer together, there's nothing like a compact car.

A man begins cutting his wisdom teeth the first time he bites off more than he can chew.

There's one thing to be said about ignorance: it causes a lot of interesting arguments.

The quickest way to get undivided attention is to make a mistake.

For fixing things around the house, nothing beats a checkbook.

Dignity is a thing that cannot be preserved in alcohol.

Those rainy days, for which a man saves, usually come during his vacation.

The man who thought nothing of walking ten miles a day now has a grandson who doesn't think much of it, either.

Never argue with your doctor. She has inside information.

The bigger things in life than money are bills.

Things could be worse. Suppose your errors were published every day like those of a baseball player.

This fishing business is simple. All you have to do is get there yesterday when the fish were biting.

A sure way to lose money is to bet on a sure thing.

Nothing makes you more tolerant of a neighbor's noisy party than being there.

It's tough on a woman who wants to make a success in business. She doesn't have a wife to advise her.

It's a terrible shock to most of us to find out that you can't economize without spending less money.

If you fool some of the people all of the time, and all of the people some of the time, don't worry. Someone else will fool them the rest of the time.

There should be a special express lane into Heaven for school bus drivers and Little League umpires.

A zombie has no mind of his own and walks around without knowing where he's going or what he's doing. In Hollywood, we call them "pedestrians." -Bob Hope

Money still talks, but with every passing year, it makes less cents.

Criticism is one of the few things people would rather give than take.

When a man and a woman marry, they become one... and, later, they discover which one.

It is a clever man who finds the wolf at the door and the next day, shows up in a fur coat.

It's nice to live in a small town, because if you don't know what you're doing, someone else does.

I read an article that said that the symptoms of stress are impulse buying, eating too much and driving too fast. Are they kidding? That's what I call a perfect day!

All reports are in. Life is now officially unfair.

A man will take out the garbage and give the impression that he's cleaned the whole house.

Men wake up looking as good as when they went to bed.

Women somehow deteriorate during the night.

Married men should forget their mistakes. There is no need for two people to remember the same thing.

No husband has ever been shot while doing the dishes.

A spotless house is the sign of a misspent life.

I love deadlines. I especially like the whooshing sound they make as they go flying by.

Tell me what you need and I'll tell you how to get along without it.

Two wrongs don't make a right; but three rights make a left.

If swimming keeps you in shape, how do you explain whales?

My reality check just bounced.

Am I getting smart with you? How would you know?

You never really learn how to swear until you learn how to drive.

To succeed in politics, it is often necessary to rise above your principles.

A Law of Life: you can't fall off the floor.

Nothing in the known universe travels faster than a bad check.

Karate is a form of martial arts in which people who have had years and years of training can, using only their hands and feet, make some of the worst movies in the history of the world.
-Dave Barry

Lazlo's Chinese Relativity Axiom: No matter how great your triumphs or how tragic your defeats... approximately one billion Chinese couldn't care less.

Writing about music is like dancing about architecture.

There's so much comedy on television. Does that cause comedy in the streets? -Dick Cavett

668: The Neighbor of the Beast

If a woman has to choose between catching a fly ball and saving an infant's life, she will choose to save the infant's life – without even considering if there are men on base.   -Dave Barry

Marriage is the only battle where you get to sleep with the enemy.

Don't cry because it's over. Smile because it happened.

I know karate, kung fu, and 47 other dangerous words.

Never invite trouble. It will accept the invitation every time.

The greatest pleasure in life is doing what people have said you cannot do.

Youth looks ahead, old age looks back, and middle age looks tired.

I know they say that love is blind, but does it also have to be deaf, dumb, and stupid?

The direct use of force is such a poor solution to any problem, it's generally used only by small children and large nations.

WIT AND WISDOM FROM DAVE BARRY

You will never find anybody who can give you a clear and compelling reason why we observe daylight savings time.

No matter what happens, somebody will find a way to take it too seriously.

You should not confuse your career with your life.

If you had to identify, in one word, the reason why the human race has not achieved, and never will achieve, its full potential, that word would be "meetings."

A person who is nice to you but rude to the waiter, is not a nice person.

There is a very fine line between "hobby" and "mental illness."

The one thing that unites all human beings, regardless of age, gender, religion, economic status or ethnic background, is that, deep down inside, we all believe we are above-average drivers.

Your friends love you anyway.

Lord, grant me the serenity to accept the things I cannot change, the courage to change the things I can, and the wisdom to hide the bodies of those I had to kill because they ticked me off.

Things are more like they are now than they ever were before. -Pres. Dwight D. Eisenhower

China is a big country, inhabited by many Chinese. -Chas. De Gaulle

The police are not here to create disorder. They're here to preserve disorder. -Chicago Mayor Daley

I've never had major knee surgery on any other part of my body. –W. Bennet, basketball player

Outside of the killings, Washington has one of the lowest crime rates in the country.
-D C Mayor Marion Barry

The internet is a great way to get on the Net.
-Republican Bob Dole

Half this game is 90% mental.
-Phillie's manager Danny Ozark

Smoking kills. And if you're killed, you've lost a very important part of your life. -Brooke Shields

That lowdown scoundrel deserves to be kicked to death by a jackass, and I'm just the one to do it.
-a Congressional candidate

The streets are safe in Philadelphia. It's only the people who make them unsafe. -Mayor F. Rizzo

I was recently on a tour of Latin America and the only regret I have was that I didn't study Latin harder in school so I could converse with these people. -Dan Quayle

It's wonderful to be here in the great state of Chicago. -Dan Quayle (again!)

It isn't pollution that's harming the environment, it's the impurities in our air and water that are doing it. -Dan Quale (yes, the same!)

The President has kept all the promises he intended to keep. –a Clinton aide

Spring ahead. Fall back. Winter in Boca.

Question Authority. Ask me anything.

THE LATE, GREAT, WONDERFULLY WITTY BOB HOPE

ON TURNING 70:

You can still chase women, but only downhill.

ON TURNING 80:

This is the time of your life when even your birthday suit needs pressing.

ON TURNING 90:

You know you're getting old when the candles cost more than the cake.

ON NEVER WINNING AN OSCAR:

Welcome to the Academy Awards, or, as it's called at my house, "Passover."

ON GOLF:

Golf is my profession. Show business is just to pay the greens fees.

ON RECEIVING THE CONGRESSIONAL GOLD MEDAL:

I feel very humble, but I think I have the strength of character to fight it.

ON HIS SIX BROTHERS:

That's how I learned to dance. Waiting for the bathroom.

Live each day as if it were your last, because someday it will be.

A practical nurse is one who marries a wealthy, terminally-ill patient.

Criticism is one of the few things people would rather give than receive.

Dignity is a thing that can't be preserved in alcohol.

If you don't believe in luck, how else do you explain the success of those you don't like?

The quickest way to get undivided attention is to make a mistake.

People who live in glass houses might as well answer the doorbell.

There's one good thing to be said about a narcissist. He doesn't talk about other people.

There's one good thing to be said about ignorance. It causes a lot of interesting arguments.

God made man before woman so man had time to think of an answer to her first question.

When I come to one of the forks in the road of life, I don't waste time and energy wishing it was a spoon. -Miss Piggy

Forget health food. I'm at an age where I need all the preservatives I can get.

As you get older, your secrets are safe with your friends because they can't remember them either.

I would be unstoppable ... if I could just get started.

Out of estrogen. Next mood swing: two minutes.

The surest way for a parent to get a teenager's attention is to sit down and look comfortable.

I live in my own little world. But it's okay; they know me here.

You can't stay young forever. But you can be immature for the rest of your life.

If you leave me, can I come too?

Funny. I don't remember being absent-minded.

It's not the pace of life that concerns me, it's the sudden stop at the end.

There are two kinds of pedestrians: the quick and the dead.

Never knock on Death's door. Ring the bell and run.

It is much easier to get older than it is to get wiser.

I tried to get a life once. They told me they were out of stock.

It's hard to make a comeback when you haven't been anywhere.

On the other hand, you have different fingers.

Those who live by the sword get shot by those who do not.

I don't suffer from insanity ... I'm a carrier!

Fifty is the ultimate F-word.

SO YOU THINK ENGLISH IS EASY? Actually, it's pretty strange.

The farm was used to produce good produce.
The bandage was wound around the wound.
The dump was so full that it had to refuse any more refuse.
We must polish the Polish furniture.
He could lead if he would get the lead out.
The soldier decided to desert his dessert in the desert.
Since there is no time like the present, we figured it was time to present the birthday present.
A bass was painted on the head of the bass drum.
When shot at, the dove dove into the bushes.
I did not object to the beautiful object.
The insurance was invalid for the invalid.
There was a row among the oarsmen about the correct way to row.
She was too close to the door to close it.
The buck does strange things when the does are around.
The farmer taught his sow how to sow seed.
The wind was too strong to wind the sail.
Upon seeing the tear in my wedding gown, I shed a tear.
I was forced to subject the subject to tests.
How can I intimate this to my intimate friend?

Let's face it: English is a crazy language. There is no egg in eggplant, nor ham in hamburter, either apple nor pine in pneapple. English muffins weren't invented in English or French Fries in France.

Sweetmeats are candies while sweetbreads, which aren't sweet, are meat. We know that quicksand works slowly; boxing rings are square; and a guinea pig is neither from Guinea nor is it a pig.

Why is it that writers write but fingers don't fing, grocers don't groce and hammers don't ham? If the plural of tooth is teeth, why isn't the plural of booth, beeth? One goose, two geese; so, one moose, two meese? One index, two indices!

And isn't it strange that you can make amends but never one amend. If you have a bunch of odds and ends and get rid of all but one of them, what do you call it? I don't know, either.

Furthermore, if teachers taught, why didn't preachers praught? If a vegetarian eats vegetables, what does a humanitarian eat? In what other language do people recite at a play and play at a recital? Ship by truck and send cargo by ship? Have noses that run and feet that smell? (And vice-versa!)

How can a slim chance and a fat chance be the same, while a wise man and a wise guy are opposites?

We have to marvel at the unique lunacy of a language in which your house can burn up as it burns down, which really burns you up. You fill in a form by filling it out; and an alarm goes off by going on. English reflects the creativity of the human race which, of course, is not a race at all. That is why, when the stars are you, you can see them; but when the lights are out, you can't see much at all.

And P.S.: how come "Buick" doesn't rhyme with "quick?"

When you do a good deed, get a receipt, in case Heaven is like the IRS.

Growing old is mandatory ... growing up is optional.

The two most common elements in the universe are hydrogen and stupidity.

You who think you know it all are damned annoying to those of us who do.

The more I learn about women, the more I love my Harley.

A man will pay $10 for a $5 item he needs. A woman will pay $5 for a $10 item she doesn't need at all, because it's on sale.

OUR MOST-USED TWO-LETTER WORD
UP

Yes, UP means toward the sky or at the top of the list, but when we get UP in the morning, we are waking UP. At a meeting, a topic comes UP for discussion. We are told to speak UP, especially if we're UP for election; but it's UP to our assistant to write UP a report.

We UP the ante in a betting game and tote UP our winnings.

We brighten UP a room by polishing UP the silver, plumping UP the pillows, cleaning UP the kitchen; and then we warm UP the leftovers for supper.

We lock UP the house and mechanics fix UP our car. A clogged drain must be opened UP because it is stopped UP. A store is opened UP for business and closed UP at night.

People stir UP trouble, line UP for tickets, work UP an appetite and think UP excuses for being late. You're always dressed if you have anything on, but being dressed UP is special.

When rain threatens, we say it's clouding UP. When the sun comes out, it's clearing UP. Too much rain can mess things UP but no rain means everything dries UP.

If you're mixed UP about UP, look it UP in the dictionary. In most dictionaries, it takes UP almost 1/4 page and can add UP to 30 definitions.

If you are UP for it, you might try building UP a list of the many ways UP is used. This chore will take UP a lot of time, but if you don't give UP, you may wind UP with a hundred or more.

We could go on and on, but let's wrap it UP for now, our time is UP, so it's time to shut UP shop.

Now it's UP to you, what you do with all this information. Chin UP, there's nowhere to go but UP.

Drinking is not a solution, unless we are talking about alcohol.

When someone tells you that nothing is impossible, ask him to dribble a football.

Life is like a cobweb, not an organizational chart. -Ross Perot

Live every day to the fullest. When going to the bathroom, take a newspaper.

Life is just a phase you're going through ... you'll get over it.

It may be that your sole purpose in life is to serve as a warning to others.

Life doesn't imitate art, it imitates very bad television. -Woody Allen

As we struggle to make sense of everything, life looks on calmly.

You know it's love when you want to keep holding hands even after you're sweaty.

The four most important words in a marriage: I'll do the dishes.

Women like cats. Men like dogs.

A woman marries a man expecting he will change; and he doesn't.

A man marries a woman expecting she will never change; and she does.

To a man, a hardware store is similar to a black hole in space. Once he goes in, he isn't coming out any time soon.

In every organization, there is one person who knows what's going on. That person must be fired.

Every morning when I get up, I look at the Forbes list of the richest people in America. If my name's not there, I go to work.

I've had a perfectly wonderful evening, but this wasn't it. -Groucho Marx

REAL WORD MEANINGS, WHEN USED BY WOMEN

1) Fine. I am right and this argument is over. You need to shut up.

2) That's okay. A dangerous phrases, when used to a man. It means she's thinking long and hard about how you will be punished for your mistake.

3) Nothing. This means "something" so be on your toes. Arguments that start with "Nothing" usually end with "Fine." (See **1**)

4) Five minutes. I she's getting dressed, this means half an hour. But don't whine; it's the same definition when you're asked to do chores.

5) Thanks. A woman is thanking you. Don't question this. Say "You're welcome" and let it go.

6) Loud sigh. Strictly speaking, not a word but a non-verbal statement often misunderstood by men. It means she thinks you're an idiot and wonders why she's standing here wastng her time, arguing with you about "Nothing." (See **3**)

7) Go ahead. Beware. This is a dare, not permission.

8) Don't worry about it. I got it. The second-most dangerous thing a woman can say. It means she has asked you several times to do something and is now doing it herself. (This will result in you asking at a later time, "What's wrong?" For her response, see **3.**

Asking if computers can think is like asking if submarines can swim.

I don't know how you feel about old age . . .but in my case, I didn't even see it coming. It hit me from the rear. -Phyllis Diller

The good thing about going to your 25-year high school reunion is that you get to see all your old classmates. The bad thing is that they get to see you. -Anita Milner

DOCTOR: Did your parents enjoy good health?
GRACIE ALLEN: Oh, yes, they loved it!

It is possible that blondes also prefer gentlemen. -Mamie Van Doren

If they can put one man on the moon... why can't they put them ALL there?

No matter who you vote for... the government gets elected.

The rings of Saturn are actually composed of lost luggage.

A seminar on time travel will be held two weeks ago.

LIMERICKS

LIMERICKS

There was a young fellow of Lyme
Who lived with three wives at one time.
When asked, "Why the third?'
He replied, "One's absurd...
And bigamy, sir, is a crime.'

♣

I knew a young lady of Hyde
Who ate some green apples and died.
The apples fermented
Inside the lamented,
And made cider inside her inside.

♣

A tone-deaf old person named Bing
When somebody asked him to sing.
        Replied, "It is odd
        But I cannot tell God
Save the Weasel from Pop Goes the King."

♣

A near-sighted fellow named Walter
Led a glamorized gal to the altar.
        A beauty he thought her
        Until soap and water
Made her look like the rock of Gibraltar.

♣

A bather whose clothing was strewed
By big winds that left her quite nude
        Saw a man come along
        And, unless we are wrong,
You expect this last line to be lewd.

♣

A handsome young monk in a wood
Told a girl she should cling to the Good.
        She obeyed him most gladly,
        He repulsed her, but sadly,
And said she had misunderstood.

♣

An amoeba named Sam and his brother
Were having a drink with each other,
In the midst of their quaffing
They split themselves laughing
And each of them now is a mother.

♣

A young man who lived in Calcutta
Had really the most awful stutta,
He said, "Pass the h...ham,
And the j...j...j...jam,
And the b...b...b...b...b...b...butta."

♣

There was a young lady of Wilts
Who walked on the Highlands on stilts.
When they said, "Oh, how shocking
To show so much stocking!"
She answered: "Well, how about kilts?"

♣

A funny old farmer from Leeds
Once swallowed a packet of seeds.
It soon came to pass
He was covered with grass
But has all the tomatoes he needs.

♣

Said a logical linguist called Rolls,
"As we always call Polish folk 'Poles,'
    For better precision
    (I am a logician)
We ought to call Dutch people 'Holes.'"

♣

A Turk named Abdullah Ben Barum
Had sixty-five wives in his harem.
    When his favorite horse died,
    "Mighty Allah!" he cried,
"Take a few of my wives...I can spare 'em!"

♣

I once knew a girl from New York
Whose body was lighter than cork.
    She had to be fed
    With a half ton of lead
Before she went out for a walk.

♣

A red-headed fellow named Rick
Liked to hit, liked to bite, liked to kick.
    Although he was bright
    He wanted to fight,
So he learned how to run really quick.

♣

A flea and a fly in a flue
Were imprisoned, so what could they do?
Let us fly said the flea,
Said the fly let us flee,
So they flew through a flaw in the flue.

♣

There was a faith healer from Deal
Who said "Although pain isn't real,
If I sit on a pin
And it punctures my skin,
I dislike what I fancy I feel."

♣

Consider your fav'rite Swiss cheese:
Why, half of it's holes, as you sees.
Now is it like that
To cut down on the fat
Or to circulate air, if you please?

♣

There once was a man from Nantucket
Who kept all his cash in a bucket.
Then his daughter named Nan
Ran away with a man
And, as for the bucket, Nan tucket.

♣

I knew a young lady named Bright
Whose speed was much faster than light.
She set out one day
In a relative way
And returned on the previous night.

♣

A silly young fellow from Clyde
In a funeral march he was spied.
When asked, "Who is dead?"
He just giggled and said:
"I don't know. I just came for the ride."

♣

A mouse in her room woke Miss Dowd
Who was frightened, it must be allowed.
Soon a happy thought hit her,
To scare off the critter.
She sat up in her bed and meowed.

♣

If Jonah had just gone to Yale
Instead of the gut of a whale,
He'd have a diploma,
A better aroma,
And a nice little co-op in Vail.

♣

It's a favorite project of mine,
A new value of pi to assign.
    I would fix it at 3,
    For it's simpler, you see,
Than 3 point 14159.

♣

A limerick fan from Australia
Regarded his work as a failure.
    His verses were fine
    Until the fourth line
And then . . . .

♣

An exceedingly fat friend of mine,
When asked at what hour he'd dine.
    Replied, "At eleven,
    At three, five, and seven,
And eight, and a quarter past nine."

♣

A young schizophrenic named Struther
Who learned of the death of his brother,
Said, "I know that it's bad
But I don't feel too sad,
After all, I will still have each other."

♣

The wonderful Wizard of Oz
Retired from his business becoz
Due to up-to-date science,
For most of his clients
He wasn't the wizard he woz.

♣

There once was a dieter named Steen
Who became so incredibly lean'
And flat, and compressed
That his back touched his chest,
And seen sideways, he couldn't be seen.

♣

There was an old man with a beard
Who said, "It is just as I feared
Two owls and a hen
Four larks and a wren
Have all built their nests in my beard!"

♣

There was a young lady whose eyes
Were unique as to color and size.
When she opened them wide,
People all turned aside,
And started away in surprise.

♣

There was an old person whose habits
Induced him to feed upon rabbits.
When he'd eaten eighteen
He turned perfectly green
Upon which he relinquished this habit.

♣

There was an old man in a tree
Who was very annoyed by a bee.
When they said, "Does it buzz?"
He replied, "Yes, it does
It's a regular brute, don't you see!"

♣

Said an ape as he swung by his tail.
To his offspring both female and male,
"From your children, my dears,
In a couple of years
May evolve a professor at Yale."

♣

Said an envious, erudite ermine,
"There's one thing I cannot determine:
When a girl wears my coat,
She's a person of note.
When it's on me, they all call me vermin."

♣

I knew a young lady called Rose
Who had a large wart on her nose.
When she had it removed
Her appearance improved,
But her glasses slid down to her toes.

♣

Do you know the great family called Stein?
There's Gert and there's Ep and there's Ein.
Gert's poems are bunk,
Ep's statues are junk,
And no one can understand Ein.

♣

There once was an old man of Esser
Whose knowledge grew lesser and lesser.
It at last grew so small,
He knew nothing at all,
And now he's a college professor.

♣

The limerick packs laughs anatomical
Into space that is quite economical.
But the good ones I've seen
So seldom are clean,
And the clean ones so seldom are comical.

♣

There was a young man from Japan
Whose limericks never would scan.
When we all asked him why,
He replied with a sigh,
"It'sbecauseItrytogetinasmanywordsasIcan."

♣

There was a young lady called Lynn
Who was so excessively thin
That when she essayed
To drink lemonade
She slipped through the straw and fell in.

♣

A good friend of mine name of Maud
Was really a terrible fraud.
She never was able
To eat at the table
But alone in the kitchen–my gawd!

♣

A critic refused, as reviewer,
To read the obscene and impure.
He soon left the scene,
For the books that were clean
Just kept getting fewer and fewer.

♣

There was a young maid from Madras
Who had the most beautiful ass.
    Not rounded and pink
    As you probably think.
It was gray, had long ears, and ate grass.

♣

A careless young lady, one Fall,
Wore a newspaper dress to a ball.
    The dress, it caught fire
    And burned her entire:
Front page, metro section, and all.

♣

A robin my cat once befriended
'Til one day the friendship was ended.
    I came home to find that
    The cat changed her mind.
From her mouth a long feather extended.

♣

I once knew a girl named Irene
Who lived on distilled kerosene.
    She started absorbin'
    A new hydrocarbon,
And since then has never benzene.

♣

The limerick is callous and crude,
Its morals distressingly lewd.
    It's not worth the reading
    By persons of breeding.
It's devised for the vulgar and rude.

♣

Now baseball is truly the ticket.
The game's so exciting and quick, it
    Never gets boring.
    Some sports have me snoring.
Like bowls, darts, golf, croquet and cricket.

♣

A fellow named Phineas Fly
Resides in a muddy pigsty.
    If you asked why this was,
    He'd reply, "Oh, because
It is none of your business, that's why!"

♣

A green-fingered lass named Veronica
Grew a prize-winning bright red Japonica.
    So how did she nourish
    The plant, make it flourish?
She played to it on her harmonica.

♣

A virile young soldier of Parma
Leapt straight into bed with his charmer.
She, naturally nude
Said, "Please don't think me rude,
But I do wish you'd take off your armor."

♣

There was a young lady from Ghent
Whose TV antenna got bent.
The neighbors went crazy
Their screens became hazy,
For, instead of receiving, she sent!

♣

A cowboy who lived in the West
Was shot sixty times in the chest.
He said, "It don't hurt,
But it's ruined my shirt,
And I'll bet you I'll need a new vest."

♣

A dancer from far Pango Pango
Is expert performing the tango
To say that his waltz
Is as good would be faltz;
But he does a half-decent fandango!

♣

There was a young man from Moosejaw
Who wanted to meet Bernard Shaw.
When asked as to why,
He made no reply;
But sharpened his circular saw.

♣

Mark Twain was a mop-headed male
Whose narratives sparkled like ale.
And this Prince of the Grin
Who once fathered Huck Finn
Can still hold the world by the tale!

♣

A surgeon of some imprecision
Decided on self-circumcision.
A slip of the knife–
"Oh, dear!" said his wife,
"Our sex life will be needing revision."

♣

A tutor who taught on the flute
Tried to teach two young tooters to toot
Said the two to the tutor,
"Is it harder to toot, or
To tutor two tooters to toot?"

♣

A girl called Miss Fortune sighed, "Oh,
My name's a misfortune, I know.
Miss Take's just as bad
And Miss Fitt is quite mad,
And that Miss B. Haviour must go!"

♣

A lonely old maid named Loretta
Sent herself an anonymous letter,
Quoting Ellis on sex,
And Oedipus Rex,
And exclaimed, "I already feel better!"

♣

A nimble young gymnast named Fritz
Did, as his finale, the splits
It raised such a laugh
As he split right in half,
And was carried away in two bits!

♣

A cheese that had plenty to say
Was walking and talking one day.
Said the cheese, "Kindly note
That my Mom was a goat,
And I'm made out of curds, by the whey!"

♣

A remorseful young glutton named Jake
Had a horribly bad stomachache.
He flopped in a chair
Saying, "It's only fair
"For I gobbled the whole chocolate cake!"

♣

Quite the worst one a Mother could pick
Was the Nanny in charge of young Nick.
She fed him mince pies,
Ice cream, chocolate, and fries,
Then complained when the poor boy was sick!

♣

A stunning young lady named Joyce
Told us "I have no R's in my voice.
But I dance wock and woll
Wear a wabbit-skin stole
And dwive in a swanky Wolls Woyce."

♣

A boy, treasure hunting, went down
To the big garbage dump outside town.
There were bedframes and cars
And old pickle jars,
And Carnegie Hall, upside down!

♣

A poor little earthworm, they say,
Was chopped in two pieces one day
By the merciless blade
Of a gardener's spade,
And the two of him wriggled away.

♣

"Our turtle has gone, did you know?"
Said a boy to his mother with woe.
"How on earth can you tell?"
"When I knocked on its shell
And said, "Are you there?" it said, "No!"

♣

There was a young woman from Potts
Who, when learning Morse Code, cried out, "What's
The matter with me?
Dashes fill me with glee–
But I can't get along with the dots!"

♣

A well-endowed lady from Bude
Went swimming one day in the nude.
From the lifeguard a shout:
"All inflatibles out!"
There was no need to be quite so rude!

♣

A lady there was in Antigua
Who said to her spouse: "What a pig you are!"
He answered, "My queen!
Is't my manner you mean
Or do you refer to my figua?"

♣

A certain young chap named Bill Beebee
Was in love with a lady named Phoebe.
"But," he said, "I must see
What the clerical fee
Be before Phoebe be Phoebe Beebee."

♣

Said the Duchess of Alba to Goya:
"Paint some pictures to hang in my foya!"
So he painted her twice:
In the nude, to look nice,
And then in her clothes, to annoya.

♣

There once was a sculptor named Phidias
Who had a distaste for the hideous;
So he sculpt Aphrodite
Without any nightie,
Which shocked all the ultra-fastidious.

♣

There was an old lady of Harrow
Whose morals were terribly narrow;
At the end of her paths,
She had built two bird baths–
For the different sexes of sparrow.

♣

A senorita who strolled on the Corso
Displayed quite a bit of her torso.
A crowd soon collected
And no one objected,
Though some were in favor of more-so.

♣

A businesslike harlot named Draper
Once tried an unusual caper.
What made it so nice,
Was you got it half-price
If you bought from her ad in the paper.

♣

There was a young girl called Bianca
Who slept while her ship lay at anchor;
She awoke with dismay
When she heard the mate say,
"Hi! Hoist up the top sheet and spanker!"

♣

A plumber from Bayswater Creek
Was called to a girl with a leak.
She looked so becoming,
That he fixed all her plumbing,
And didn't emerge for a week.

♣

Though most Enterprise men are whites,
Uhura has full equal rights.
Her crewmates, you see,
Love de-moc-ra-cy,
And the way that she fills out her tights.

♣

There was a young lady called Etta
Who fancied herself in a sweater.
Three reasons she had.
Keeping warm was not bad,
But the other two reasons were better.

♣

I knew a young lady called Lynn
Who thought fornication a sin.
But when she was tight,
She thought it all right,
So the fellows, they filled her with gin.

♣

Up the street sex is sold by the piece,
And I wish that foul traffic would cease.
It's a shame and improper,
And I'd phone for a copper,
But that's where you'll find the police.

♣

There was a trombonist called Herb
Whose playing was loud, though superb.
When neighbors complained,
Young Herbert exclaimed:
"But great art is meant to disturb."

♣

As Mozart composed a sonata,
The maid bent to fasten a garter.
Without any delay
He started to play
Un poco piu apassionata.

♣

There was an old man who averred
He had learned how to fly like a bird.
Cheered by thousands of people,
He leapt from the steeple...
This tomb states the date it occurred.

♣

A daring young woman from Guam
Observed, "The Pacific's so calm.
I'll swim out for a lark."
Well, she met a large shark...
Let us now sing the Ninetieth Psalm.

♣

Consider the Emperor Nero
Of many lewd tales he's the hero.
Though he scraped on the fiddle,
He just couldn't diddle
And his real batting average was zero.

♣

God's plan had a hopeful beginning
But Man spoilt his chances by sinning.
We trust that the story
Will end in great glory
But at present, the other side's winning.

♣

There was a young lass of Australia
Who went to the dance as a dahlia;
When the petals unfurled.
It revealed to the world
That the dress, as a dress, was a failure.

♣

There was an old hermit named Dave
Who kept a dead whore in his cave.
He said, "I admit
I'm a bit of a twit,
But just look at the money I save!"

♣

There was a young poet of Kew
Who failed to emerge into view
So he said, "I'll dispense
With rhyme, meter, and sense."
And he did, and he's now in Who's Who.

♣

A famous theatrical actress
Played best in the role of malefactress.
Yet her home life was pure,
Except, to be sure,
A scandal or two, just for practice.

♣

On the chest of a barmaid in Yale
Were tattoo'ed the prices of ale.
And on her behind
For the sake of the blind
Was the same information in Braille.

♣

Archimedes, the well-known truth seeker
Jumping out of his bath, cried "Eureka!"
He ran half a mile,
Wearing only a smile,
And became the world's very first streaker.

♣

There once was an artist named Saint
Who swallowed some samples of paint.
All shades of the spectrum
Flowed out of his rectum,
With a colorful lack of restraint.

♣

There once was a man from Bombay
Who wore on his head a toupee.
He thought that he might
Give his friends a delight
And go shiny and bald for a day.

♣

An epicure dining at Crewe
Found a very large bug in his stew.
Said the waiter, "Don't shout
And wave it about,
Or the rest will be wanting one too."

♣

There was a young hunter named Shepherd
Who was eaten for lunch by a leopard.
Said the leopard, "Egad!"
You'd be tastier, lad,
If you'd only been salted and peppered!"

♣

A lovely young man from Great Britain
Interrupted two girls at their knittin'.
Said he with a sigh,
"That park bench...well, I
Just painted it where you are sittin'"

♣

I knew a nice fellow named Wyatt
Whose voice was exceedingly quiet.
And then it, one day,
Just faded away...
....

♣

I knew an announcer called Herschel
Whose habits became controversial.
Because when out wooing,
Whatever was doing,
At ten, he'd insert his commercial.

♣

There once was a young kid named Darren
Whose room was surprisingly barren.
He had so few toys
Unlike most normal boys,
Because he was so into sharin'.

♣

Should you find yourself in prosecution,
Your lawyers will find resolution.
If the plaintiffs should score,
From your guts and your gore,
Hope your net worth is not the solution.

♣

Don't eat sweets, brush your teeth, and floss more.
All behaviors that dentists adore.
If we did what they say
Would we need them? No way!
Makes you wonder what dentists are for!

♣

If your partner is seeking divorce,
That's a matter for lawyers, of course.
Is your ex feeling mean?
Is she trying to clean
Out your savings and every resource?

♣

In a castle that had a deep moat
Lived a chicken, a duck and a goat.
They wanted to go out
And wander about,
But couldn't, for lack of a boat.

♣

There was a dear lady of Eden
Who on apples was quite fond of feedin'.
She gave one to Adam
Who said, "Thank you, Madam."
And instantly started in breedin'.

♣

An unfortunate deaf mute from Kew
Was trying out songs that were new.
He did them so fast,
That his fingers at last
Got tangled, and fractured a few.

♣

The limerick's callous and crude,
Its moral distressingly lewd;
It's not worth the reading
By persons of breeding
It's designed for us vulgar and crude.

♣

There was a young girl from St. Cyr
Whose reflex reactions were queer.
Her escort said, "Mabel,
Get up off the table!
That money's to pay for the beer!"

♣

A girl who was no good at tennis,
When swimming was truly a menace.
She took pains to explain,
"It depends how you train.
I was once a street-walker in Venice."

♣

An elderly man name of Keith
Mislaid his old set of false teeth.
They'd been laid on a chair,
He'd forgot they were there,
Sat down...and was bitten beneath.

♣

There was a young lady named Maris
Whom nothing could ever embarrass
'Til the salts that she shook
In the bath that she took
Turned out to be Plaster of Paris.

♣

An opera star named Mariah
Always tried to sing higher and higher,
'Til she hit a high note
Which got stuck in her throat,
And she entered the Heavenly Choir.

♣

"My girlfriend would like me to ski,"
Said the flabby young cellist, "But, gee,
With StravinSKY, StokowSKI,
MussorgSKY, TchaikovSKY,
That's quite enough SKIing for me."

♣

There was a young fellow at Trinity,
Who, although he could trill like a linnet, he
Could never complete
Any poem with feet,
Saying: "Idiots
Cannot you see
What I'm writing just happens to be
Free
Verse?

♣

JUST JOKES

JUST JOKES

Two women meet in Heaven.

Sylvia: Hi, Wanda!

Wanda: Hi, Sylvia! How'd you die?

Sylvia: I froze to death.

Wanda: How horrible!"

Sylvia: It wasn't so bad. After I quit shaking from the cold, I began to get warm and sleepy and drifted into a peaceful death. How about you?

Wanda: I had a massive heart attack. I suspected my husband was cheating, so I snuck home to catch him in the act. But, instead, I found him sitting in the den, watching tv.

Sylvia: So what happened?

Wanda: I was so sure he was cheating, I ran all over the house looking for that woman. I ran up to the attic and down to the basement, went through every closet and checked under all the beds. Finally, I was so exhausted, my heart gave out and I died.

Sylvia: Too bad you didn't look in the freezer... we'd both still be alive.

A college class was told to write a short story in as few words as possible. The story had to contain (1) religion; (2) sex; and (3) mystery.

The only story that got an A+ is this one:

"Oh God, I'm pregnant. I wonder who did it?"

*****

Don was driving to a very important meeting and couldn't find a parking space anywhere. Looking heavenward, he said, "Lord, if you'll find a spot for me to park, I promise I'll go to church regularly every Sunday for the rest of my life, and I'll give up drinking, too."

Miraculously, a parking space appeared. Don looked up again, saying, "Never mind, I found one."

* * * * *

An older gentleman had an appointment to see the urologist. He approached the desk behind which sat a very grim-looking woman. He gave her his name. In a very loud voice, she said, "YES, I HAVE YOUR NAME HERE. YOU WANT TO SEE THE DOCTOR ABOUT IMPOTENCE, ISN'T THAT RIGHT?"

Every head in the room snapped around to stare at the embarrassed man.

But in an equally loud voice, he replied: "NO, I'VE COME TO INQUIRE ABOUT A SEX CHANGE OPERATION. BUT I DON'T WANT THE SAME DOCTOR THAT DID YOURS."

The room erupted in applause.

"Ough" can be pronounced in nine different ways. Here they are in one sentence:

"A tough-coated, dough-faced, thoughtful ploughman strode through the streets of Scarborough; after falling into a slough, he coughed and hiccoughed."

* * * * *

I was sitting in the waiting room for my first appointment with a new dentist.

When I read his diploma on the wall, I suddenly recalled a tall, handsome dark-haired boy with the same name, who had been in my high school class some 40-odd years ago. What a crush I had on him! Could this be the same person?

Upon seeing him, however, I quickly discarded any such thought. This balding, paunchy man with the deeply lined face was far too old to have been my classmate. Or was he? I just had to find out for sure.

After he examined my teeth, I asked if he had attended Morgan High School.

"I certainly did," he said with pride.

"When did you graduate?" I asked.

"In 1964. Why do you ask?"

"You were in my class!"

He peered at me for a moment.

And then that ugly old S.O.B. asked:

"Really? What did you teach?"

A drunk staggers out of a bar. The first person he sees, he says, "I'm Jesus Christ." "No, you're not." So he walks up to another man. "I'm Jesus Christ," he says. "No, you're not," is the answer. "I'll prove it," says the drunk. "Please come with me."

They all walk into the bar and the bartender says, "Jesus Christ, you again?!"

* * * * *

Wife: I think Rover is becoming a bit deaf."

Husband: Nonsense! He hears just fine. Sit, Rover! Oh dear, I guess you're right. I'll get a shovel and clean it up right away."

* * * * *

The professor looks over his class of Freshmen and says sarcastically: "If there are any idiots in this room, please stand up." Nobody moves for several minutes; then one boy stands.

So tell us," says the teacher, "why do you consider yourself an idiot?"

"Actually, I don't," says the boy, "but I didn't want you to be standing there all alone."

* * * * *

A woman was mowing her lawn when she accidentally cut off her cat's tail. She rushed her cat, and its tail, over to the new Super Wal-Mart. Why Wal-Mart? It's the largest retailer in town.

During a visit to my doctor, I asked her, "How do you know whether or not an older person should be put in an old age home?"

"Well," she said, "we fill up a bathtub, then we offer a teaspoon, a teacup and a bucket to the person, to empty the bathtub."

"Oh, I get it," I said. "A normal person would use the bucket as it's the biggest."

"No," she said. "A normal person would pull the plug. Would you like a bed by the window?"

* * * * *

A little old lady calls her neighbor and says, "Please come over and help me. I have a killer jigsaw puzzle, and I can't figure out how to start."

Her neighbor asks, "What's it supposed to be when it's finished?"

"According to the picture on the box, it's a rooster."

The neighbor goes over and is shown the puzzle spread all over the table. He studies the pieces for a moment, then looks at the box, then turns to her and says,

"First of all, no matter what we do, we're not going to be able to assemble those pieces into anything like a rooster..."

He takes her hand and says, "Secondly, I want you to relax. Let's have a nice cup to tea and then...

"Let's put all the corn flakes back in the box."

Ed and Elaine met on vacation and Ed fell head over heels in love. They spent every minute of the next two weeks together. And so, on their last night of vacation, the two of them went to dinner and had a serious talk about their relationship.

"It's only fair to warn you, I'm a total golf nut," Ed told Elaine. "I eat, sleep, breathe and dream golf... so if that's going to be a problem, we'd better end it now."

Elaine took a deep breath and said, "Since we're being honest, here goes: you need to know that I'm a hooker."

"I see," Ed replied. He looked down for a moment, deep in thought. Then, he said, "You know it's probably because you're not keeping your wrists straight when you tee off."

* * * * *

I go to the doctor for my yearly exam. She starts with the basics. "How much do you weigh?" she asks. "145," I say. She puts me on the scale and says it's actually 170. "Your height?" she asks. "Five foot ten," I say. She measures me and says I'm 5'8". She then takes my blood pressure and tells me it's very high.

"Of course it's high!" I yell. "When I came in here I was tall and slim; now I'm short and fat!"

She put me on Prozac. What a bitch!

One day my husband decided to wash his sweatshirt. Seconds after he stepped into the laundry room, he yelled, "What setting do I use on the washer?"

"It depends," I replied. "What does it say on your shirt?"

He yelled back: "Syracuse University!"

* * * * *

Wife asks husband: "How many women have you slept with?"

Husband proudly replies: Only you, darling ... With all the others, I was awake."

* * * * *

The Italian says, "I'm tired and thirsty. I must have wine."

The Frenchman says, "I'm tired and thirsty. I must have cognac."

The Russian says, "I'm tired and thirsty. I must have vodka."

The German says, "I'm tired and thirsty. I must have beer."

The Mexican says," I'm tired and thirsty. I must have tequila."

The Jew says, "I'm tired and thirsty. I must have diabetes."

* * * * *

You're never too old to learn something dumb.

Q: Why do scuba divers always fall backwards off the boat? A: If they fell forwards they'd still be in the boat.

* * * * *

A woman was helping her husband set up his computer. At the appropriate point in the process, the computer advised him to enter a password. The husband was feeling rather clever so he picked one, spelling it out so his wife wouldn't miss it: P..E..N..I..S.

His wife fell off her chair laughing when this message appeared on the screen: PASSWORD REJECTED. NOT LONG ENOUGH.

* * * * *

A three-year-old boy is sitting on the toilet. His mother thinks he's been in there too long and she goes to see what's up. The little boy is gripping the toilet seat with one hand and hitting himself on top of his head with the other.

His mother says, "Sweetie, are you all right? You've been in here a very long time."

He says, "I'm good, Mommy. I just haven't gone poopy yet."

"Okay," says his mother. "You can stay a while longer. But why are you hitting yourself on the head like that?"

He says: "Works for ketchup."

An angry Asian lady at the bank was trying to exchange yen for dollars. "Why it change?" she demanded. "Yesterday, I get two hunt dolla for yen. Today, only hunat eighty. Why it change?"

The teller shrugged and said, "Fluctuations."

The lady says, "Fluc you white people, too!"

* * * * *

An elderly man saw people stealing things from his backyard shed. He called the Police who asked: "Is someone in your house?"

"No, but people have broken into my shed and are stealing from me."

"All patrols are busy," said the dispatcher. "Lock your doors and an officer will be along when one is available."

The man waited for a few minutes, then called again.

"I just called you because people were stealing from my shed but don't worry. I shot them both and the dogs are eating them." He hung up.

Within five minute, four Police cars, a SWAT team and two fire trucks with a paramedic showed up. They caught the burglars.

One of the cops said, "I thought you said you'd shot them."

Replied the man: "I thought you said there was nobody available."

* * * * *

A blind man found a piece of matzoh. He ran his fingers over it and said, "Who wrote this crap?"

* * * * *

Jake was dying. His wife sat at the bedside. He looked up and said weakly, "I have something I must confess."

"There's no need for that," said his wife.

"No," he insisted. "I want to die in peace. I have a confession to make. I'm so ashamed! I slept with your sister, your best friend, her best friend, and your mother!"

"I know," she replied. "Now just rest and let the poison work."

** * * *

Gallagher opened the morning newspaper and was dumbfounded to read in the obituary column that he had died. He quickly called his best friend, Finn. "Did you see the paper, Finn? They say I died." "I saw it," said Finn. "And where are you calling from?"

* * * * *

An elderly man, driving not so well, is stopped by police around 1:00 AM and asked where he is going this time of night.

"Officer, I am going to a lecture about alcohol and the effects it has on the human body."

"Really? Who is giving this lecture so late?"

The man replies, "My wife."

80-year-old Bessie bursts into the rec room at the local retirement home.

She holds her clenched fist in the air and announces: "Anyone who can guess what's in my hand can have sex with me tonight!"

At first, there is nothing but silence. Then, from the back of the room: "An elephant?"

She thinks a moment and then says, "Close enough!"

* * * * *

On Rosh HaShana morning, Rose went to wake her son. It was time to go to the synagogue.

"I'm not going!" he said.

"Why ever not?"

"I"ll give you two good reasons, Mother," he said. "One, they don't like me and two, I don't like them." Rose replied, "I'll give you two good reasons why you must go to the synagogue. One, you're 54 years old and, two, you're the Rabbi."

* * * * *

Her husband was slipping in and out of consciousness.

"Come here," he whispered. "I have something to say to you."

She sat on the bed and held his hand. "When I was shot, you were at my side. When they arrested me for fraud, you waited for me. When my business failed, you stayed with me. And now I'm dying, and here you are, by my side. You know what, sweetheart?"

"What, darling?" she breathed.

"I think you're very bad luck."

A doctor on his morning walk, noticed a very elderly woman sitting on her front porch. She was bent and totally wrinkled; yet she was smoking a cigar and smiling! He walked up to her and said, "I couldn't help noticing how contented you look. What's your secret?"

"Ten cigars a day," she said. "Before bed, I smoke a nice big joint. Apart from that, I drink a whole bottle of Jack Daniels every week and eat only junk food. On weekends, I pop a few pills and get laid. Forget exercise!"

"That is absolutely amazing! How old are you?"

"Thirty-four," she replied.

* * * * *

A senior citizen driving on US1 gets a frantic phone call. His wife cries, "I just heard that there's a car going the wrong way on US1!"

"Not just one," he replies. "There are hundreds of them!"

* * * * *

A guy walks into a bar, orders 12 shots of whisky and belts them back as fast as he can.

The bartender asks why he's drinking so much, so fast.

"You'd drink if you had what I have."

"And what do you have?"

"Seventy-five cents."

* * * * *

Gravity isn't my fault. I voted for Velcro.

An elderly couple went to a restaurant and were told that, since they had no reservation, there would be a wait of 45 minutes.

""Young man," said the husband. "We're both 90 years old. We may not have 45 minutes."

They were seated immediately.

* * * * *

A blonde teenaged girl wanted to earn some money over the summer. She started canvassing a well-to-do neighborhood.

At the front door of the first house, the owner said, "Well, I could use somebody to paint my porch. How much do you want for that?"

"How about $50?"

The man agreed and got the brushes and paint out of the garage.

"You didn't tell her the porch went all around the house," the man's wife said.

"She didn't ask," he replied. "You know what they say about dumb blondes." They both laughed.

Later that day, the girl came to the door to collect her money.

"You're finished already?"

"Yes," she replied, "and I even used the leftover paint to put on a second coat."

Impressed, the man gave her $50 plus a $10 tip.

"And by the way," the blonde added, "It's not a Porch, it's a Lexus."

* * * * *

If only we'd stop trying to be happy, we could have a pretty fine time. -Edith Wharton

A little old lady at the old age home was running around, flipping up her nightgown and crying: "Supersex! Supersex!"

She stopped at a man in a wheelchair and, flipping up her nightgown, said, "Supersex!"

After a moment of thought, he said:

"I'll have the soup."

* * * * *

Last night, my kids and I were sitting in the living room and I said to them, "I never want to live in a vegetative state, dependent on some machine and fluids from a bottle. If that ever happens, just pull the plug." They got up, unplugged the computer, and threw out my wine, the little idiots!

* * * * *

An old Italian grew delicious tomatoes but this year, he was stiff with arthritis and the ground was very hard. His son Vincent, who used to help him, was in jail. The old man wrote him a letter: Dear Vincent, it looks like I won't be able to plant my tomato garden this year. If only you were here, you could do the heavy digging for me. Love, Papa."

A few days later, he got a letter from his son. "Dear Pop, Don't dig up that garden. It's where the bodies are buried. Love, Vinnie."

Early the next morning, the FBI and police arrived and dug up the entire area; but they found nothing. Apologizing to the old man, they left. That same day, he got another letter from his son:

"Dear Pop. Go ahead and plant your tomatoes now. That's the best I could do under the circumstances. Love you, Vinnie."

A father asked his 10-year-old son if he knew about the birds and the bees. "I don't want to know!" the boy said. "Please don't tell me!" The confused father asked what was wrong.

The boy said, "When I was six, you told me there's no Easter Bunny. At seven, you told me there's no Tooth Fairy. At eight, you hit me with the 'there's no Santa' speech.

"If you're going to tell me that grownups don't really get laid, I'll have nothing left to live for!"

* * * * *

One day a man and his wife were discussing anger management. He said to her, "When I get mad at you, you never fight back. How do you keep it all inside?"

She said, "I clean the toilet bowl."

He asked, "How does that help?"

With a serene smile, she said, "I use your toothbrush."

* * * * *

A wife says to her husband, "Would you please go to the store and get me one carton of milk and if they have eggs, get six."

A short time later, the husband comes back with six cartons of milk.

The wife says, "Why in the world did you get six cartons of milk?"

He replies: "They had eggs."

IN MEMORIUM: Let us take a moment to reflect upon the death of Larry LaPrise, the man who wrote "The Hokey Pokey." He died peacefully at the age of 93. The most traumatic part for his family was getting him into the coffin.

They put his left leg in. And then the trouble started.

* * * * *

The commanding officer of a Marine regiment decided to pose a tricky question to all assembled for the morning briefing.

"How much of sex is work and how much is pleasure?"

The executive officer said 75-25 in favor of work. A captain said it was 50-50, and an aide responded with 25-75 in favor of pleasure.

One young PFC said, "Sir, it has to be 100% pleasure. If there was any work involved, the officers would have me doing it for them."

* * * * *

The woman applying for a job in a Florida lemon grove seemed far too qualified for the job, given her Ivy League degree and her former jobs as social worker and teacher. The foreman frowned at her application and said, "I have to ask you this: have you had any experience in picking lemons?"

"Well, as a matter of fact, yes. I've been divorced three times."

Bill Gates reportedly compared Microsoft to Ford. "If Ford had kept up with technology like the computer industry has, we would all be driving $25 cars that get 1,000 miles to the gallon."

To which Ford issued a press release saying: "If Ford had developed technology like Microsoft, your car would crash for no reason--twice a day. Then, every time they repainted the lines in the road, you would have to buy a new car. You'd have to press the Start button to turn the engine off.

"Occasionally your car would just die on the highway. You'd have to pull to the side of the road, close all the windows, turn off the car, restart it, and reopen the windows before you could continue. For some reason, you would accept this as normal.

"Sometimes, making a left turn would cause your car to shut down and refuse to restart; and you would have to reinstall the engine. All warning signals would be replaced by a single 'This car has performed an illegal operation' warning light. Every time a new model was introduced, drivers would have to learn how to drive all over again because nothing would work the same.

"If you chose Macintosh, you would get a car powered by the sun, five times as fast and twice as easy to drive. But it would run on only 5% of the roads in the world. We'd like to add that if you wanted customer service, you'd get someone in a foreign country and be told how to fix the car yourself."

Just before the funeral services, the undertaker came up to the very elderly widow and asked, "How old was your husband?"

"98," she replied. "Two years older than me."

"So you're 96," the undertaker commented.

She said, "Hardly worth going home, isn't it?"

* * * * *

I've sure gotten old! I've had two bypass surgeries, a hip replacement, and new knees. Fought prostate cancer and diabetes.

I'm half blind, can't hear anything quieter than a jet engine, take 30 different medications. Have bouts with dementia and terrible circulation. Can't remember if I'm 85 or 92. I've lost all my friends.

But thank God, I still have my Driver's License!

* * * * *

I'm a woman of a certain age and I felt that my body had gotten totally out of shape. I got my doctor's permission to join a fitness program and I picked an aerobics class for seniors.

I bent, and I twisted, and I gyrated, jumped up and down and perspired for an hour.

But by the time I got my tights on, the class was over!

* * * * *

Money is how talentless people keep score.

A man of middle years drove his brand-new Corvette convertible out of the dealership and, once on the road, pushed it to 80, enjoying the wind blowing through his hair. "Amazing!" he thought, as he flew down I-95, pushing the pedal even more.

Looking in his rearview mirror, he saw the State Trooper behind him, blue lights flashing and siren blaring. He floored it to 90, then 100, then 110. Then he came to his senses.

"What am I doing?" he said to himself. "I'm too old for this!" and he pulled over.

The Trooper leaned in the window, looked at his watch, and said, "Sir, my shift ends in 20 minutes. Today is Friday. If you can give me a reason for speeding I've never heard before, I'll let you go without a ticket."

The driver paused, thinking, and then said, "Three years ago, my wife ran off with a State Trooper. I thought you were bringing her back."

"Have a good day, sir."

* * * * *

A woman found a bottle on the beach and was amazed when a huge blue genie appeared. "You have one wish," he said. She said, "I want peace in the Middle East to last forever." "That's impossible, lady! I can't do that! No genie could!" "Okay," she said, "then find me a perfect man."

The genie sighed. "Show me that map again."

HEAVEN IS WHERE:
The Police are British
The Chefs are Italian
The mechanics are German
The lovers are French ... and it's all organized by the Swiss.
HELL IS WHERE:
The Police are German
The Chefs are British
The mechanics are French
The lovers are Swiss ... and
It's all organized by the Italians.

* * * * *

A HAPPY LIFE:
It's important to have a woman who helps at home, cooks, cleans up, and holds a job.
It's important to have a woman who can make you laugh.
It's important to have a woman you trust.
It's important to have a woman who is good in bed, and loves being with you.
And it's very very important that these four women do not know each other.

* * * * *

A husband says to his wife, "What would you do if I won the lottery?" "I'd take half and leave," she replies. "Good. I just won $12. Here's $6 and you can start packing any time now."

The owner of a small deli was being questioned by an IRS agent about his tax return.

"Why don't you people leave me alone?" he lamented. I work like a dog, the place is closed only three days a year, my entire family works with me, and you want to know how I made $80,000 for the year?"

"It's not your income; it's these deductions," said the agent. "Six trips to Bermuda?"

"Oh, I forgot to tell you. We deliver."

* * * * *

Dr. Green goes into a bookstore and asks the young female clerk, "Do you have the new book for men with short penises? I can't remember the title." She replies, "I'm not sure it's in yet."

Says the doctor: "That's the one! I'll take two copies."

* * * * *

A farmer was driving along a road with a truckload of manure. A little boy, playing in front of his house, called out, "What's in your truck that smells so bad?

"Fertilizer," said the farmer.

"What are you going to do with it?"

"Put it on my strawberries."

"You should come and live with us," the little boy said. "We eat ours with sugar and cream."

A customer asks: "Where could I find some Polish sausage?"

The clerks says, "Are you Polish?"

The man, clearly offended, says, "Well, as a matter of fact, I am. But let me ask you: if I had asked where is the bratwurst, would you think I'm German; if I wanted kosher hot dogs, would you assume I'm Jewish; and if I wanted mortadella, would you think I had to be Italian?"

"No," admits the clerk. "I wouldn't."

"So why did you ask me if I'm Polish just because I asked for Polish sausage?"

"Because you're at Home Depot."

* * * * *

The sheriff in a small Western town arrested a young blond cowboy for walking down the main street buck naked. As he locked him up, he asked: "How come you're not wearing any clothes?"

"It's like this, Sheriff," said the cowboy. "I'm at the bar down the road and this pretty little redhead gal invites me to her motor home... so I went. We go inside and she pulls off her top and asks me to take off my shirt ... so I did. Then she pulls down her skirt and says I should pull off my pants... so I did. Then she takes off her undies and says I should do the same ... so I did.

Then she gets on the bed and says, 'Now go to town, cowboy.' And here I am!"

Son of a gun. Dumb blond guys do exist.

The husband had just finished reading a book called You Are the Master of Your House. He announced to his wife: "From now on, you need to know that I am the master in this house and my word is law. You will prepare me a gourmet meal tonight and when I'm finished, you will serve me a sumptuous dessert. After dinner, you will go upstairs with me and we will have sex until I say 'Stop.' Then you will draw me a bath, scrub my back, towel me dry, and bring me my pj's. Then, tomorrow, guess who's going to dress me and comb my hair?"

"The funeral director would be my first guess."

* * * * *

A senior citizen was on the operating table, awaiting surgery. He had insisted that his son, a well-known surgeon, perform the operation his way. Before the anesthesia, he motioned to his son.

"Yes. Dad. What is it?"

"Just do your best, son; don't be nervous... and remember, if I should die, your mother is going to come and live with you and your wife."

* * * * *

5,000 men were asked to complete a survey on what they liked best about oral sex.

3% liked the warmth.

4% enjoyed the sensation.

93% appreciated the silence.

An Amish boy and his father were visiting a mall. They were amazed by everything; but especially by two shiny silver walls that could move apart and back together.

"What is that, Father?"

The father, never having seen an elevator in his life, responded: "I've never seen anything like it and I admit I don't know what it is."

While they stood there, an old lady in a wheelchair rolled up to the moving walls and pushed a button. The walls opened and she rolled into a small room. The walls closed and the father and son watched the small circular numbers above the walls light up sequentially until they got to the top.

The numbers began to light up in reverse order, and, as they watched in wonderment, the walls opened up again and a beautiful young woman stepped out.

The father, without taking his eyes off the young woman, said quietly to his son: "Go get your mother."

* * * * *

Into a bar walked an Italian, a Swiss, a German, a Frenchman, an American, a Canadian, an Ethiopian, a Zulu, a Cambodian, an Israeli, an Egyptian, a Dutchman, a Serbian, a Russian, a Pole, an Irishman, a Brit, an Indian and a Czech.

The bouncer says, "I'm sorry. I can't let you in without a Thai."

An Irishman, a Mexican, and a blonde guy were doing construction work on scaffolding on the 20th floor of a building in Chicago.

They stopped to eat lunch and the Irishman said, "Corned beef and cabbage! If I get corned beef and cabbage one more time for lunch, I'm going to jump off this building!"

The Mexican opened his lunch box and exclaimed, "Burritos, again! If I get Burritos one more time, I'm going to jump off, too!"

The blond opened his lunch and said, "Bologna again! If I get a bologna sandwich one more time, I'm jumping, too!"

The next day, the Irishman opened his lunch box, saw corned beef and cabbage, and jumped to his death.

The Mexican opened his lunch, saw Burritos, and jumped, too.

The blond guy opened his lunch, saw bologna and jumped to his death, as well.

At the funeral, the Irishman's wife was weeping. "If I'd only have known how tired he was of corned beef and cabbage, I'd never have given it to him again!"

The Mexican's wife also wept and said, "I could have given him tacos or enchiladas! I didn't know he hated Burritos so much."

Everyone looked at the blond guy's wife.

She said, "Don't look at me! He made his own lunch!"

HIS AND HER DIARY FOR THE SAME DAY:

HER: Tonight, I think my husband fell out of love with me. We had made plans to have dinner at a nice restaurant. He hardly greeted me, although I was quite a bit late; and he only picked at his food. I asked him what was wrong and he said, "Nothing," but I know that isn't true. On the way home, I told him that I love him and he just smiled a little and kept driving. Why didn't he say, "I love you, too?" I'm so upset. When we got home he stayed distant, not speaking, just watching TV. Finally, with silence all around us, I went to bed and began to cry. When he came up five minutes later, he didn't even notice, just changed and climbed into bed, turning his back. I just know he has fallen for someone else! My life is a disaster!

HIM: Boat wouldn't start, can't figure out why.

* * * * *

Oh boy, am I rich! Silver in the hair, gold in the teeth, crystals in the kidneys, sugar in the blood, and an inexhaustible supply of natural gas!

* * * * *

Judge Judy to prostitute: "When did you realize you had been raped?"

Prostitute: (wiping away tears) "When the check bounced!"

An older man walked into a jewelry store on a Friday evening with a beautiful young girl and asked to see the jeweler's best diamond ring.

The jeweler brought out three rings. "Here's a stunner for only $10,000," he said. "Not good enough," said the customer. "How about the square cut for $15,000?" "Not good enough," was the answer.

"This one is over four carats, set in platinum and surrounded by 3 carats in smaller stones. It is $25,000."

The girl's eye sparkled. The old gentleman said, "We'll take it. I know you need to make sure my check is good, so I'll write it now and you can call the bank first thing Monday to verify the funds and then I'll pick up the ring that afternoon."

Monday morning, the jeweler phoned the customer. "Sir, there's no money in that account."

"I know," said the old man, "but let me tell you about my weekend!"

* * * * *

A distraught senior citizen phoned her doctor's office. "Is it true," she wanted to know, "that the medication you prescribed has to be taken for the rest of my life?"

""Yes, I'm afraid so," the doctor answered.

After a moment, she said, "Doctor, please tell me the truth about what I have... because this prescription is marked 'NO REFILLS.'"

Traveling along a highway, I stopped at a service station and headed to the ladies' room. There were two cubicles and one was already in use.

No sooner did I close the door when I heard: "Hi, how are you?"

I don't know what got into me, but I answered, somewhat embarrassed: "Doin' fine."

The other woman says, "So what are you up to these days?"

Thinking that this is too bizarre, I say, "Um, like you, just traveling."

Now I'm nervous and trying to get out fast, when I hear: "Can I come over?"

Very weird. "No, I'm a little busy right now," I say, preparing to make a quick exit.

Then I hear her say nervously, "Listen, I'll have to call you back. There's a crazy lady in the other cubicle who keeps answering my questions."

* * * * *

I read one psychologist's theory that said, "Never strike a child in anger." When could I strike him? When he's kissing me on my birthday? When he is recuperating from the measles? Do I slap the bible out of his hand on a Sunday?"

-Erma Bombeck

* * * * *

What's so great about freedom? It's just chaos but with better lighting.

A minister decided that a visual demonstration would punch up his Sunday sermon.

Four worms were placed into four different jars. The first worm was put into a container of alcohol. The second worm was put into a container filled with cigarette smoke. The third worm was put into a container of chocolate syrup. The fourth worm was put into a container of good clean soil.

At the conclusion of his sermon, the minister reported the following results:

The first worm in alcohol–dead.

The second worm in cigarette smoke–dead.

The third worm in chocolate syrup–dead.

The fourth worm in good clean soil–alive.

So the minister asked his congregation, "What did you learn from this demonstration?"

A man who was sitting in the back quickly raised his hand and said, "As long as you drink, smoke, and eat chocolate, you won't have worms!"

* * * * *

Jeff just found out his wife is pregnant. According to her due date, Jeff was out of town at the time of conception. He couldn't believe it. He would finally make it into the Guinness Book of Records for impregnating his wife with phone sex!

* * * * *

Ask me about my third chromosome.

A guy walks into a bar and says to the barman: "Give me six double vodkas."

The barman says, "Wow, you must have had one hell of a day."

"Yeah, I just found out my eldest son is gay."

The next day, the same guy comes into the bar and, again, asks for six double vodkas.

When the barman asks what the trouble is this time, he says, "I just found out my youngest son is gay, too."

On the third day, the guy comes into the bar and orders yet another six double vodkas.

The bartender says, "Jesus, doesn't anyone in your family like women?"

The man downs his first drink and shakes his head. "Yeah," he says. "My wife."

* * * * *

Adam and Eve had an ideal marriage. He didn't have to hear about all the men she should have married.

And she didn't have to hear about his mother's great cooking.

* * * * *

Moses, returning from Mt. Sinai, spoke to the people.

"The good news is that we got them down to ten.

"The bad news is, adultery is still in."

A blonde wanted to go ice fishing. She'd seen many books on the subject. After finally getting all the necessary tools together, she made for the ice.

After positioning her comfy footstool, she started to make a circular cut in the ice.

Suddenly, from the sky, a voice boomed: "THERE ARE NO FISH UNDER THE ICE!"

Startled, the blonde moved her gear further down the ice, poured a thermos of cappuccino, and began again to cut a hole. Again the voice bellowed: "THERE ARE NO FISH UNDER THE ICE!"

The blonde, now concerned, moved once more, down to the opposite end of the ice and once again started to cut her hole.

Once more the voice boomed, "THERE ARE NO FISH UNDER THE ICE!" She stopped, looked skyward, and said, "Is that you, Lord?"

The voice replied: "NO, THIS IS THE MANAGER OF THE HOCKEY RINK!"

* * * * *

A blind man walks into a bar with his seeing-eye dog. He stands in the middle of the room, takes the dog by his chain and starts swinging the animal above his head.

Everyone stops what they're doing and stares. One patron, upset about what he sees, runs up to the blind man, and shouts, "What the hell are you doing?"

The blind man says, "Just looking around."

The woman, a recent immigrant from Argentina, is driving on a major highway. She gets pulled over by the highway patrol.

The officer says, "Ma'am, do you realize you were speeding?"

The woman doesn't speak English well so she asks her husband in Spanish, "What did he say?"

Her husband says, in Spanish, "You went above 150 km."

The patrolman says, "May I see your license and registration, please?"

The woman asks her husband again,"What did he say?" Her husband translates.

The woman finds the papers and hands them to the cop, who says, "I see you are from Argentina. I spent some time there once, had the worst sex I ever had with a woman."

The woman turns to her husband. "What did he say?"

The husband replies, "He says he knows you."

* * * * *

A woman was trying hard to get the ketchup out of the bottle. During her struggle, the phone rang and she asked her 4-year-old daughter to answer.

"It's the minister, Mommy," the little girl said. Then she added, into the phone, "Mommy can't come to the phone right now. She's hitting the bottle."

A trucker came into a truck stop café and placed his order: "I want three flat tires, a pair of headlights and a pair of running boards."

The brand-new blonde waitress, not wanting to appear stupid, went into the kitchen and asked the cook what that meant. "What does he think this place is: an auto parts store?"

The cook explained: Three flat tires mean three pancakes, a pair of headlights is two eggs sunny side up, and running boards are two slices of crisp bacon."

"Okay," said the waitress. She thought about it for a moment and then spooned up a bowl of beans and gave it to the trucker.

"What are the beans for, Blondie?"

She replied, "I thought while you were waiting for the flat tires, headlights and running boards, you might as well gas up."

* * * * *

A dog thinks:

Hey, these people I live with feed me, love me, provide me with a nice warm dry house, pet me and take care of me. They anticipate my every need. They must be Gods!

A cat thinks:

Hey, these people I live with feed me, love me, provide me with a nice warm, dry house, pet me and take good care of me. They anticipate my every need. I must be a God!

An older couple was having dinner one evening when the husband said, "Emma, soon we will be married 50 years and there's something I have to know. Have you been unfaithful to me?"

After a moment, Emma replied, "Well, Irving, I have to be honest. Yes, I've been unfaithful to you three times during these nearly 50 years, but always for a good reason."

Irving, hurt, said, "I never suspected. Can you tell me what you mean by a 'good reason?'"

"The first time was shortly after we were married and we were about to lose our little house because we couldn't pay the mortgage. Do you remember that one evening I went to see the banker and the next day he notified you that the loan would be extended?"

Irving did recall and said, "I can forgive you for that. You saved our home. But what about the second time?"

"Do you remember when you were so sick but we didn't have the money to pay for the heart surgery you needed? Well, I went to see your doctor one night and, if you recall, he did the surgery at no charge."

"And you did it to save my life, so of course, I can forgive you for that. Now tell me about the third time."

"All right," said Emma. "So do you remember when you ran for president of the synagogue and you needed 43 more votes?"

A guy walks into a bar and asks the bartender if he'll give him a free beer for an amazing trick. The bartender agrees. The guys pulls out a hamster that begins singing and dancing on the bar .

"That is amazing," says the barman, and gives him a beer. "If I show you something even more amazing, will you give me another beer?" The bartender agrees.

The guy pulls out a small piano and a frog. The same hamster plays the piano while the frog dances on the bar and sings.

The barman, completely wowed, gives him another beer.

A man in a suit, who's been watching the entire time, offers to buy the frog for $100 and the man agrees. "Are you nuts?" cries the bartender. "You could make a fortune off that frog... and you let him go for a mere one hundred bucks?"

"Can you keep a secret?" says the man. "That frog is a fraud. The hamster's a ventriloquist."

* * * * *

On the first day of school, a first-grader handed his teacher a note from his mother. The note read: "The opinions expressed by this child are not necessarily those of his parents."

* * * * *

When I was a girl, I had only two imaginary friends; and they would only play with each other.

A little boy got lost at the health club and found himself in the women's locker room. When he was spotted, the room burst into shrieks, with ladies grabbing towels and running for cover.

The child watched in amazement and then said, "What's the matter? Haven't you ever seen a little boy before?"

* * * * *

A guy is sitting at home when he hears a tiny knock on his door. There's a snail on the porch, which he picks up and throws as far as he can.

Three years later, another tiny knock. The same snail is there. The snail says, "What the hell was THAT about?"

* * * * *

A panda walks into a restaurant, orders the special, eats it, then pulls out a pistol, kills the waiter, and starts to walk out the door.

The owner accosts him, saying, "What in the world were you thinking?"

Says the panda, "Look it up in the dictionary."

In the dictionary, under Panda, it reads:

Panda: black and white animal; lives in central China; eats shoots and leaves.

* * * * *

You have the right to be silent, so, please SHUT UP!

A drunk is driving through the city, his car weaving all over the road. Eventually, he's pulled over by a cop.

"Did you know," says the officer, "that a few intersections back, your wife fell out of the car?"

"Oh, thank heavens," says the drunk. "For a minute there, I thought I'd gone deaf."

* * * * *

A husband and wife were involved in an argument, both of them unwilling to give in.

"I'll admit I was wrong," the wife said after a while, in a conciliatory attempt, "if you'll admit that I'm right."

He agreed and, like a gentleman, let her go first. "I'm wrong," she said. With a twinkle in his eyes, he said, "You're right!"

* * * * *

A blonde and her husband are lying in bed, trying to sleep, but failing because the next-door neighbor's dog is out in the yard, barking and barking and barking.

She jumps out of bed and says, "I've had enough of this!" And she runs downstairs.

Finally, the blonde comes back to bed and her husband says, "The dog is still barking. What did you do?"

She says, "I put the dog in our yard. Let's see how THEY like it!"

A little girl asked her mother, "How did the human race appear on the earth?"

Her mother replied, "God made Adam and Eve and they had children and their children had children, and so on. And that's how humans began."

A few days later, the little girl asked her father the same question, and he answered: "Many millions of years ago, there were apes from which the human race evolved."

The confused girl returned to her mother and said, "How come you say humans came from God and Daddy says they came from apes?"

"It's really very simple, sweetie. I told you about my side of the family and your father told you about his."

* * * * *

The aspiring psychiatrists were attending a class on emotional extremes.

"Let's establish what we're talking about," said the professor. To a student from New York, he said, "What's the opposite of joy?" "Sadness," said the student.

"And the opposite of depression?" to a student from California. "Elation," said she.

"And you, sir," he said to the young man from Texas. "How about the opposite of woe?"

The Texan replied, "Sir, I believe that would be giddy-up."

My wife and I were strolling on Main Street when we saw a traffic cop putting a ticket on a rather old car with a license plate that read AARP.

"Come on, officer," I said. "Give a senior citizen a break, why don't you?"

He ignored me, so my wife called him a Nazi. He glared at her and started to write a second ticket, so I told him he was a shithead. Two tickets went under the wiper and a third one was started. So we threatened to report him to the ACLU. Immediately, ticket number four was whipped out.

This went on for many minutes and the tickets kept piling up.

Personally, we didn't care. We came into town by bus.

* * * * *

A man walking out of a bar late at night has had a few too many. He walks down the street with one foot on the sidewalk and one in the gutter. It looks awkward and he's having a hard time of it.

A policeman comes up to him and says, "Well, sir, I see you have had one too many to drink."

"I have?" replies the man. "By God, I have! Oh thank the Lord. I thought I was crippled!"

* * * * *

Married men revealed that they perform the following act twice as often as single men:

Change their underwear!

Jesus came across a woman crouching in a corner, the crowd around her preparing to stone her to death for adultery.

Jesus held up his hand and said, "Let he who is without sin cast the first stone."

A woman at the back of the crowd fired off a good-size stone at the adulteress. At which point, Jesus looked over and said, "Mother! Sometimes, you really piss me off!"

* * * * *

MORTAL: What is a millions years like to you, oh God?"

GOD: Like one second.

MORTAL: What is a million dollars like?

GOD: One penny.

MORTAL: Can I have a penny?

GOD: Just a second..."

* * * * *

Consumption of alcohol may create the illusion that you are tougher, handsomer and smarter than some really really big guy named Tony. It may lead to you think that people are laughing WITH you. It may lead you to think that you're a really nifty ballroom dancer.

* * * * *

Marriage is a three-ring circus: an engagement ring ... a wedding ring . . . and suffering.

Two nuns are given the job to paint a room that is being redecorated in honor of the Pope's coming visit. Mother Superior tells them they must not get one drop of paint on their habits. So they decide to paint in the nude.

In the middle of the project, there comes a knock on the door. "Who is it?" calls one of the nuns.

"It's the blind man," says the voice from the other side of the door.

The two nuns look at each other and shrug, deciding that no harm can come from letting a blind man into the room. They open the door.

"Nice tits," says the man. "Where do you want the blinds?"

* * * * *

A student comes to a young professor's office. She glances down the hall, closes his door, comes close to him at the side of his desk.

"I would do anything to pass this exam."

She leans closer to him, flips back her hair, gazes meaningfully into his eyes.

"I mean," she whispers, "I would do ANYTHING."

He returns her gaze. "Anything?"

"Yes," she says. "Anything."

His voice turns to a whisper. "Would you ... study?"

Six retired guys in Florida had a regular poker game in their condo clubhouse. While playing one afternoon, Dan lost $500 on a single hand, clutched his chest, and dropped dead at the table.

Showing respect for their fallen comrade, the other five continued playing, but standing up.

At the end of the game, Rich looks around and says, "So, who's going to tell his wife?"

They cut the cards. Steve picks the low card and has to carry the news. They tell him to be discrete, be gentle, don't make a bad situation any worse.

"Don't worry," Steve says. "Discretion is my middle name. Leave it to me. I'll handle it."

Steve goes to Dan's condo and knocks on the door. The wife calls though the door, asking what he wants.

Steve says: "Your husband just lost $500 at poker and is afraid to come home."

"Tell him to drop dead!" yells the wife.

"I'll go tell him right away," says Steve.

* * * * *

MORE STEPHEN WRIGHT:

Why do psychics have to ask for your name?

How do you know when you run out of invisible ink?

Bills travel through the mail at twice the speed of checks.

I'd kill for a Nobel Peace Prize.

Typical macho man married typical pretty lady and after the wedding he laid down his rules:

"I"ll be home when I want, if I want and at what time I want–and I don't expect any hassle from you. I expect a great dinner to be on the table unless I tell you that I won't be home for dinner. I'll go hunting, fishing, boozing and card-playing whenever I want with my old buddies and don't you give me a hard time about it.

"Those are my rules. Any comments?"

His new bride said, "No, that's fine. Just understand that there will be sex here at 7:00 o'clock every night ... whether you're here or not."

* * * * *

A doctor and his wife were having a fight at the breakfast table. The husband got up in a rage and said, "What's more, you're no good in bed either!" and stormed out of the house.

After a few hours, he realized he probably shouldn't have said that. He called home to apologize.

After many rings, his wife finally picked up the phone and her husband, now irritated, said, "What took you so long to answer?"

"I was in bed."

"In bed, this early? Whatever for?" said the doctor.

"Getting a second opinion!"

An elderly couple decided it was time to take a class to improve the memory. They learned how to remember things by association with other, more familiar, things.

A few days after the class, the husband was talking outside with a neighbor. "Where was the class given?" asked the neighbor.

"Oh... ummmm..." the old man pondered. "You know that flower, the one that smells so nice, but has thorns all over, what's the name of that flower?" "A rose?" the neighbor suggested.

"Yes, that's it!" He turned toward his house and shouted: "Hey, Rose, what was the name of the place where we took that memory class?"

* * * * *

God is tired, worn out. He speaks to St. Peter. "I need a vacation," he says. "Got any suggestions?" St. Peter says, "How about Jupiter. It's nice and warm on that planet this time of year."

God shakes His head, saying, "No, too much gravity. You know how that hurts my back."

St. Peter reflects. "How about Mercury?"

"Too hot!"

"I've got it!" says St. Peter, his face lighting up. "How about visiting Earth for a few millenia?"

"Are you kidding?" says God. "Two thousand years ago I went there, had an affair with a nice Jewish girl, and they're still going on about it."

A man, sick of the outside world joins a temple in Tibet. One of the rules in this most holy order is that he is allowed to say only two words every five years.

The first five years he eats rice, he sleeps on a wooden bed and has only one blanket with holes. He tends to the fields and looks after livestock every day.

After five years, the head monk comes to him and says he may use his two words.

"More blankets," he says. Now the man is warm at night but still eats only rice and tends to the fields and livestock every day.

Another five years pass and the head monk comes to him again to say he may use two more words.

"More food," he replies.

He now is warm at night and eats gourmet food every day but he still has his jobs outside.

Another five years and the head monk comes again to tell him he may use his two words.

"I'm leaving," replies the man.

"Good," says the head monk. "All you've done since you came here is complain."

* * * * *

A young woman who drove from Memphis to Florida in a convertible and was surprised when she arrived sunburned. She didn't think this could happen if the car was moving.

A scientist doing research work in the rain forests of South America comes upon a three-foot-tall pygmy standing proudly near a 7,000-pound elephant, stone cold dead.

The scientist exclaims: "Good grief! Did you actually kill this beast?"

"Oh yes," replies the pygmy.

"But it's so huge and you're so small!"

"Still, you see that it's dead."

"How on earth did you kill it?"

"With my club," replied the little man.

"How big is your club?" asked the scientist, full of wonder.

The pygmy replied, "Well, I figure there are about a hundred of us."

* * * * *

The teenager had just received his brand-new driver's license and, to celebrate, the whole family got into the car for his inaugural drive. Dad immediately headed for the back seat, directly behind the newly-minted driver.

"I'll bet you're back there to get a change of scenery after all those months of sitting in the front seat, teaching me how to drive," said the son.

"Nope," said Dad.

"I'm gonna sit back here and kick the back of your seat while you drive, just like you've been doing to me for sixteen years."

A man was attempting to ride his bicycle from Phoenix to the Grand Canyon. He made it across the desert without incident, but when he reached the mountains, the steep grade gave him trouble. He decided to hitchhike for a while

Some time later, a car offered him a lift, but said, "Your bicycle won't fit in the car." So he opened the trunk, took out a piece of rope and tied one end of the rope to his bumper and the other end to the bike. "If I go too fast, honk your horn and I'll slow down," he said.

This scheme worked well for several miles, until another car zoomed past. Not to be outdone, the car with the bike attached took off.

Both cars zoomed through a speed zone and a trooper's radar gun clocked them traveling at 120 mph. The trooper radio'ed ahead to another officer and said, "You're got two vehicles headed your way, both doing over 120 mph."

"Thanks, buddy."

The first trooper hesitated a moment, then added: "You're not going to believe this ... there's a guy following on a bicycle and he's honking to pass!"

* * * * *

Three ministers having lunch were discussing how to get rid of bats in the belfry. They had tried everything: noise, cats, spray, loud radios. Nothing seemed to work. Then one pastor said: "I baptized all of my bats. Haven't seen one back since!"

A man calls the hospital, frantic: "My wife is in labor and her contractions are only two minutes apart!"

"Is this her first child?" asks the operator.

"No, this is her husband!"

* * * * *

A blonde sees a letter lying on her doormat. On the envelope, it says DO NOT BEND. She spends the next hour trying to figure out how to pick the thing up.

* * * * *

Q: What's the difference between men and pigs?

A: Pigs don't get drunk and act like men.

* * * * *

An old farmer's dog goes missing and he's very sad. His wife suggests he put an ad in the local paper. He does so, but two weeks go by and there are no calls.

"What did you put in your ad?" asks the wife.

"Here, boy!"

* * * * *

Buddhism for beginners: Deep inside you are 10,000 flowers. Each flower blossoms 10,000 times. Each blossom has 10,000 petals.

You might want to see a specialist.

Barney's in jail. A guard looks in and sees him hanging by his feet.

"What in hell are you doing?" he asks.

"Hanging myself."

"The rope should be around your neck."

"I know," says Barney. "But I couldn't breathe."

* * * * *

A blonde goes to the vet with her goldfish. "I think it's got epilepsy," she tells the vet.

Vet takes a look and says, "It seems calm enough to me."

She says, "I haven't taken it out of the bowl yet."

* * * * *

Muhammad Ali was once asked by a young man what he should do with his life. The boxer's reply was: "Stay in college, get the knowledge. And stay there until you're through. If they can make penicillin out of moldy bread, they can sure make something out of you!"

* * * * *

Breathe in.

Breathe out.

Breathe in.

Breathe out.

Forget this and attaining Enlightenment will be the least of your problems.

Barney's in jail. A guard looks in and sees him hanging by his feet.

"What in hell are you doing?" he asks.

"Hanging myself."

"The rope should be around your neck."

"I know," says Barney. "But I couldn't breathe."

* * * * *

A blonde goes to the vet with her goldfish. "I think it's got epilepsy," she tells the vet.

Vet takes a look and says, "It seems calm enough to me."

She says, "I haven't taken it out of the bowl yet."

* * * * *

Muhammad Ali was once asked by a young man what he should do with his life. The boxer's reply was: "Stay in college, get the knowledge. And stay there until you're through. If they can make penicillin out of moldy bread, they can sure make something out of you!"

* * * * *

Breathe in.

Breathe out.

Breathe in.

Breathe out.

Forget this and attaining Enlightenment will be the least of your problems.

A customer in the produce section of the supermarket asked to buy half a head of lettuce. The boy working there told him they sold only whole heads of lettuce; but the man insisted that the boy check with his manager. In the manager's office, the boy said, "Some butthead wants to buy a half head of lettuce." He felt someone behind him and there was the customer. Quickly, the boy added: "But this gentleman kindly offered to buy the other half."
It was agreed and the man left satisfied.

Later, the manager said to the boy, "I was impressed with the way you got yourself out of a bad situation. We like workers who can think on their feet. Where are you from, son?"

"Kansas," said the boy.

"Why did you leave?"

"Well, sir, there's nothing down there but whores and football players."

"Really?" said the manager. "My wife's from Kansas."

"No joke!" said the boy. "Who'd she play for?"

* * * * *

Getting rid of a man without hurting his pride can be a problem. Try saying, "I love you, I want to marry you and have your children."

Sometimes they leave skid marks.

* * * * *

Out of Body. Back in 5 minutes.

Recently, the U.S. Supreme Court ruled that the state of Missouri could not discriminate against the Ku Klux Klan if they wanted to participate in the adopt-the-highway program.

While the Court found the KKK an unpleasant group, the decision was a victory for free speech and equal protection under the law.

The Department of Transportation in Missouri figured out a sweet revenge. True, they could not remove the KKK's sign; but they did have the right to rename the highway.

The KKK is now regularly cleaning up a stretch of the newly-named Rosa Parks Freeway.

* * * * *

Men are forgetful, whereas women remember everything. That's why men need instant replays in sports. They've already forgotten what happened.

* * * * *

Male menopause is a lot more fun than female. With female menopause you get hot flashes and gain weight. Males get to date young women and drive motorcycles.

* * * * *

Hurrying to drive my daughter to school, I made an illegal right turn. "Uh-oh," I said. "I just made a mistake.' "No, I think it's all right," she said. "The police car behind us did the same thing."

A golfer stood over his tee shot for what seemed an eternity, measuring distance, testing the wind...and driving his partner crazy.

Finally the exasperated partner said, "What's taking so long? Just hit the damn ball!"

His friend explained, "My wife is up there watching me from the club house. I want to make this a perfect shot."

"Give me a break! You don't stand a snowball's chance in hell of hitting her from here!"

* * * * *

Two 90-year-old women, Selma and Margie, were lifelong friends. When Margie was dying, Selma visited her every day. One day, she said, "Margie, we played softball all through High School and all through college. We played in a women's league in town for years. Do me a favor, please. When you get to Heaven, somehow get word to me if there's a women's softball team there." Her friend agreed and within days, she died. A week later, Selma was awakened late at night by a lightning flash. "Selma, it's me, Margie. I have some good news and a little bad news." "Tell me," said Selma. "I can take it."

"Yes, there's a women's softball team in Heaven, and all our old buddies are on it. It's always Spring up here and we can play forever." "That's great," Selma said. "And the bad news?"

"You're pitching on Tuesday."

A successful rancher died and left everything to his devoted wife. She was a smart and good-looking woman, determined to keep the ranch going. However, she knew very little about how to run a ranch, so she placed an ad in the paper for an experienced ranch hand. Two cowboys applied. One was gay and the other, a drunk.

She thought long and hard and–when no one else applied–decided to hire the gay guy. He proved to be very knowledgeable and a hard worker. For weeks, the two of them worked together, and the ranch was doing very well.

One day, the widow told the hired hand, "You've done a really good job. I am pleased. You should go into town and kick up your heels this Saturday." He readily agreed, saying he'd be home
at midnight. Midnight came and went, 1:00 o'clock, then 2:00, then 3:00 AM and no hired hand. He finally returned around 3:30 and found the widow sitting by the fireplace with a glass of wine, waiting for him. She quietly called him over to her.

"Unbutton my blouse and take it off," she said. Trembling, he did so. "Now, take off my boots." He complied. "And now, my stockings." He did as she asked, placing them neatly by her boots. "Now take off my skirt and my bra." Again, he did as he was told and dropped the clothing to the floor.

She took a sip of her wine, looked him in the eye, and said, "If you ever wear my clothes into town again .... you're fired."

My five-year-old son squealed with delight when he opened his birthday present from his grandmother. It was a water pistol. He promptly ran to the sink to fill it.

"Mom," I said. "I'm surprised at you. Don't you remember how we used to drive you crazy with water pistols?"

My mother smiled. "Yes, I remember."

* * * * *

A boss asked one of his employees, "Do you believe in life after death?

"Yes, sir."

"That's what I thought," said the boss. "Yesterday after you left to go to your grandmother's funeral, she stopped in to see you."

* * * * *

A prospective son-in-law was asked by his girlfriend's father, "Son, can you support a family?"

"Well, no, sir," he replied. "I was just planning to support your daughter. The rest of you will have to fend for yourselves."

* * * * *

Late one night, a mugger jumped in front of a man and said, "Give me all your money." Indignant, the man replied, "You can't do this. I'm a United States Congressman." To which the mugger replied: "In that case give me back MY money."

OIL CHANGE INSTRUCTIONS FOR WOMEN:
1. Pull up to Jiffy Lube when the mileage reads 3,000 miles since the last oil change.
2. Drink a cup of coffee while the men work.
3. Fifteen minutes later, scan credit card and leave, driving a properly-maintained vehicle.

Money spent: oil change: $30.00 ... coffee: $1.50. Total: $31.50

OIL CHANGE INSTRUCTIONS FOR MEN:
1. Wait until Saturday, drive to auto parts store and buy a case of oil, filter, kitty litter, hand cleaner and a scented pine tree. Scan credit card for $50.00
2. Stop by beer store and buy a case: $24.00.
3. Drive home, park, open a beer and drink it.
4. Spend 30 minutes looking for jack stands. Find them under kid's pedal car. Jack truck up.
5. Open another beer and drink it.
6. Place drain pan under engine.
7. Look for 9/16 box end wrench.
8. Give up and use crescent wrench.
9. Unscrew drain plug.
10. Drop drain plug in pan of hot oil; splash hot oil on yourself in process. Cuss.
11. Crawl out from under truck to wipe hot oil off of face and arms. Throw kitty litter on spilled oil.
12. Have another beer while watching oil drain.
13. Spend 30 minutes looking for oil filter wrench.
14. Give up. Crawl under truck and hammer a screwdriver though oil filter and twist off.

15. Crawl out from under truck with dripping oil filter, splashing oil everywhere from holes you made.
16. Cleverly hide old oil filter among trash to avoid environmental penalties. Have a beer.
17. Install new oil filter making sure to apply a thin coat of oil to gasket surface.
18. Dump first quart of fresh oil into engine.
19. Remember drain plug from step 9 and 10.
20. Hurry to find drain plug in drain pan. Drink beer.
21. Discover that first quart of fresh oil, now on the floor. Throw kitty litter onto oil spill.
22. Get drain plug back in, with only minor spill. Have another beer.
23. Crawl under truck, getting kitty litter into eyes. Wipe eyes with oily rag used to clean drain plug. Slip while using stupid crescent wrench to tighten drain plug and bang knuckles on frame, removing any excess skin between knuckles and frame.
24. Begin cussing fit.
25. Throw stupid crescent wrench.
26. Cuss for additional 5 minutes because wrench hit truck and left a big dent. More beer.
27. Clean hands and bandage as required to stop blood flow.
28. Beer.
29. Dump in five fresh quarts of oil.
30. Lower truck from jack stands.
31. Move truck back to apply more kitty litter to fresh oil spilled during any missed steps.
32. Beer.

33. Test drive truck.
34. Get pulled over and arrested for driving under the influence.
35. Truck impounded.
36. Call loving wife, make bail.
37. Twelve hours later, get truck from impound yard.

Money spent:	Parts: $50.00
DUI: $2,500.00	Impound fee: $75.00
Bail: $1,500.00	Beer: $20.00
Total: $4,145.00	

BUT YOU KNOW THE JOB WAS DONE RIGHT!

* * * * *

Late one evening, I was awakened by the ringing of my phone. Sleepily, grumpily, I said Hello. There was a moment's pause and then, all in a tumble, a girl spoke: "Mom, this is Susan and I'm sorry I work you but I had to call because I'm going to be a little late. Dad's car got a flat and it's not my fault so don't be mad, honest, I don't know what happened, but please, don't be mad, okay?'

I have no daughters.

"I'm sorry, dear," I said, "but this is a wrong number. I don't have a daughter named Susan."

A pause. "Gosh, Mom," the girl said, "I didn't think you'd be <u>this</u> mad!"

* * * * *

I feel like a million–but one at a time.

The director of a local winery was looking for a new taster. A ragged dirty fellow who looked and sounded drunk came to apply for the job. The director figured he would pretend to let the man apply and he would do so badly, there would be no problem sending him on his way.

He was given a glass to taste. He said, "Muscat, three years old, grown on a North slope, matured in large old barrels. Low grade, but acceptable."

It was 100% on target. The boss was astonished. He poured another glass.

"Cabernet, eight years old, SW slope, new oak barrels, matured at eight degrees. Requires three more years for best result."

Again, right on the money. Unbelievable, thought the director. A third glass was offered.

"Non-vintage Pinot champagne, high grade and exclusive."

The director was dumbfounded. He winked at his secretary to suggest something and she left the room, coming back with a glass of urine. The drunk took a sip. "It's a blonde, 26 years old, three months pregnant, and if you don't give me the job, I'll name the father."

* * * * *

One Sunday, a child was acting up during the 10 o'clock Mass. As her father carried her up the aisle, she cried out : "Pray for me! Pray for me!"

And God created Woman and she had three breasts.

And Woman complained, saying, "Lord, I am not made to birth litters. I need but two breasts."

And God said, "Thou sayest wisely."

There was a bolt of lightning, a lingering odor of ozone and lo, it was done; and God stood holding the extra breast in his hands.

"What are you going to do with that worthless boob?" asked Woman.

And so it was that God created Man.

* * * * *

President Reagan asked his wife, Nancy, how he should choose his vice president. Nancy gave him a riddle to use as a test, saying that if one of the contenders was able to answer it, he should have the job.

Reagan asked Bush: "Who is it who is your father's son, but not your brother?"

Bush replied, "That's a hard one. I'll have to go and think on it." He was back that same evening, happily shouting: "I got it! I figured it out! It's me! It's me!"

The same riddle was then presented to the other hopeful, who also asked for time to figure it out. That evening, he returned and said, "I tried and tried, but I couldn't figure it out. Who is it?"

Reagan answered, "It's George Bush, but I 'm not exactly sure why."

The Pope is in New York for a United Nations Conference. He is running late. As he leaves the airline terminal he gets into a cab, saying, "I have to be at the UN building in ten minutes."

"Ten minutes! It takes at least forty minutes and that's with no traffic jams. I can't do it."

'Well, then, get out and let me drive," says the Pope. The cabbie is pretty nervous about this but, hey, it's the Pope. How to say no?

The Pope is enjoying the experience, dodging in and out of lanes, going about 75 miles an hour, when he zooms past a New York cop.

The cop leaps on his motorbike and pursues the speeding vehicle.

Finally, he gets the cab to pull over and when the driver puts down the window, the cop gets on his radio for assistance.

"This is road patrol and I need some help."

"What's up?"

"I've pulled someone over for speeding and he's very big. What should I do?"

"How big is he? The Mayor?"

"No, bigger than that."

"Tom Cruise? Brad Pitt?"

"Bigger than a movie star!"

"Hell, not the President!"

"Bigger than that," says the cop.

"Bigger than the President? Who the hell is it?"

"I don't know," says the cop. "But he's got the Pope driving him."

A Frenchman, an Englishman, and a New Yorker are captured by a fierce tribe in the Amazon. The chief tells them, "The bad news is, we're going to kill you and use your skins to build a special canoe. The good news is that you get to choose how you want to die."

The Frenchman says, "Poison, s'il vous plait." The chief gives him a cup of poison, the Frenchman says, "Vive la France," and drinks it down.

The Englishman says, "A pistol for me, thank you very much." He is given a pistol, points it at his head, cries, "God save the Queen!" and blows his brains out.

The New Yorker says, "Gimme a fork." The chief is puzzled but he finds a fork and forks it over. The New Yorker takes the fork and starts jabbing himself all over–chest, sides, stomach, arms, legs. He's bleeding all over the place. The chief is appalled and shouts, "What are you <u>doing?</u>"

The New Yorker sneers at the chief, and says, "So much for your special canoe, shmuck!"

* * * * *

A man wasn't feeling well so he went to the doctor. After seeing him, the doctor took his wife aside and said, "Your husband is not going to make it unless you take very good care of him, do everything for him, and be there for him 24/7." On the way home, the husband said, "What did he tell you?"

"He said you probably won't make it."

I was signing the receipt for my credit card purchase when the clerk noticed that I had never signed the back of the credit card. She informed me that she couldn't complete the transaction unless the card was signed. When I asked why, she explained that it was necessary to compare the signature on the credit card with the signature on the receipt. So I signed the credit card right then and there as she watched.

She carefully compared the two signatures. As luck would have it, they matched.

* * * * *

When my cousin Linda worked in an art supply store, she sold artists' canvas by the yard, either 36" or 48" wide. A customer came in asked asked: "Can you please cut some canvas for me?" "Certainly," said Linda. "What width?" The customer stared at her, somewhat annoyed, then said, "Scissors?"

* * * * *

Two elderly ladies, friends since their 30s, still got together several times a week to play cards. One day they were playing gin rummy and one of them said, "Please don't get mad, but for the life of me I can't remember your name. Please tell me what it is." Her friend glared at her. She continued to glare in silence for several minutes.

Finally, she said, "How soon do you need to know?"

I was in the 10 item express lane at the supermarket, quietly fuming. The woman ahead of me, oblivious to the sign, had pushed into the checkout line, her cart piled high with groceries.

Imagine my delight when the cashier beckoned the woman to come forward, looked into the cart, and sweetly asked: "So...which ten items would you like to buy?"

* * * * *

A man and his wife, in their 60's, were celebrating a wedding anniversary. On that special day, a good fairy came to them and said that because they had been so good and loyal, each one could have one wish.

The wife wished for a trip around the world with her husband. Whoosh! Instantly she had airline and cruise tickets in her hands.

The husband wished for a female companion 30 years younger. Whoosh! Instantly he turned 90.

You gotta love that fairy!

* * * * *

A man went to church one Sunday. Afterward he stopped to shake the preacher's hand. He said, "I tell you, that was a damn fine sermon! " The preacher said, "Thank you sir, but I'd rather you didn't use profanity." Said the man, "I was so damned impressed, I put five thousand dollars in the plate!" The preacher said, "No shit!"

Three sisters aged 92, 94, and 96, shared a house together. One evening, the 96 year old sister went upstairs to take a bath. As she put her foot into the tub, she paused. Then she yelled down to her sisters, "Was I getting into the tub or out of it?"

"You darn fool," shouted the 94 year old. "I'll come up and see." When she got halfway up the stairs, she paused. "Am I going up the stairs or down, does anyone know?"

The 92 year old sister was sitting at the kitchen table with a cup of tea and she thought, "I hope I never get that forgetful, knock on wood." She shook her head and called out, "I'll be up to help you both as soon as I see who's at the door!"

* * * * *

One night, an 87-year-old woman came home from Bingo to find her 92-year-old husband in bed with another woman. She became violent and ended up pushing him off the balcony of their 20th-floor apartment, killing him instantly.

Brought before the court, on the charge of murder, she was asked if she had anything to say in her own defense.

"Your Honor," she said, "I figured that if, at 92, he could screw, then he could fly!"

* * * * *

If you don't learn to laugh at trouble, you won't have anything to laugh at when you're old.

Some 15-year-old girlfriends decided to meet for dinner. They discussed where to eat and finally agreed on McDonald's next to the Sea Side Restaurant because they had only $6.50 between them and Bobby Bruce, the cute boy in science class, lived on that street.

Ten years later, the same girlfriends, now 25, agreed to meet at the Sea Side Restaurant because it had free snacks, there was no cover charge, the beer was cheap, and there were lots of cute guys.

Ten years after that, the same friends, now 35, discussed where to meet and decided on the Sea Side because the combos were good, it was near the gym, and if they went late enough, there wouldn't be noisy little kids.

Ten years later, the 45 year olds decided on the Sea Side because the martinis were big and the waiters wore tight pants.

At 55, their choice was the Sea Side because the prices were reasonable, the wine list was good, and fish was good for their cholesterol.

When they were 65, they opted for the Sea Side because there was an Early Bird Special and the lighting was good.

At 75 years of age, they once again decided to go to the Sea Side Restaurant because it was handicap accessible and the food wasn't too spicy.

Ten years later, the girlfriends, now 85, agreed to meet at the Sea Side Restaurant because they'd never been there before.

THE PERKS OF BEING OVER 60

1. Kidnappers are not very interested in you.

2. In a hostage situation, you are likely to be released first.

3. No one expects you to run ...anywhere.

4. People call at 9 P.M. and ask, "Did I wake you?"

5. People no longer view you as a hypochondriac.

6. There is nothing left to leave the hard way.

7. Things you buy now won't wear out.

8. You can eat dinner at 4:00 P.M.

9. You can live without sex (alhough not without your glasses.)

10. You no longer think of speed limits as a challenge.

11. You get into heated arguments about pension plans.

12. You sing along with elevator music.

13. You quit trying to hold your stomach in, no matter who walks into the room.

14. Your eyes won't get much worse.

15. Your joints are more accurate meteorologists than the national weather service.

16. Your secrets are safe with your friends, because they can't remember them either.

17. You can't remember who sent you this list.

And please notice, these are all in Big Print for your convenience.

A busload of American tourists in Holland stopped at a cheese farm. A young guide led them through the process of cheese making, explaining that goat's milk was used. She showed the group a lovely hillside where many goats were grazing.

"These," she explained, "are the older goats put out to pasture when they no longer produce." She then asked, "What do you do in America with your old goats?"

To which a spry old gentleman answered, "They send us on bus tours."

* * * * *

This guy is sitting at home alone, reading a book, when he hears a knock on the front door.

There are two sheriff's deputies standing there. He asks if there is a problem.

One of the deputies asks if he is married. He says that he is.

"May we see a picture of your wife?"

"Sure," the guy says. He shows them a studio photo of his wife.

The deputy says, "I'm sorry, sir, but it looks like your wife's been hit by a truck."

The guy says, "I know. But she has a great personality and is an excellent cook."

* * * * *

When I was a child, our family was so poor that all I got on my birthday was a year older.

Eric was on his deathbed and gasped pitifully, "Give me one last request, dear."

"Of course, Eric," said his wife.

"Six months after I die," he said, "I want you to marry Jonathan."

"But I thought you hated Jonathan!" she said.

With his last breath, Eric said, "I do."

* * * * *

On opening his new store, a man received a bouquet of flowers. He was dismayed when he read the card, which said, "Deepest Sympathy." Just then, his phone rang. It was the florist, apologizing for having sent the wrong card.

"I'm a businessman," said the storekeeper. "I understand how these things happen. Don't think any more about it."

"But," said the florist, "I sent <u>your</u> card to the funeral party."

"What did it say?"

"Congratulations on your new location."

* * * * *

The professor poses the following problem to one of his classes:

A wealthy man dies and leaves ten million dollars. One-fifth goes to his daughter; one-fifth to his son, one-sixth to his brother; and the rest to his wife. Now, what does each get? After a long silence, a voice from the back: "A lawyer?"

Ethan, 9 years old, visiting his grandmother, had been playing outside with the kids next door, when he came in and asked her, "Grandma, what's that called when two people sleep in the same bedroom and one is on top of the other?" Taken aback, she decided to tell the truth. "Well, dear, that's called 'sexual intercourse.'"

Ethan went back out to play and a few minutes later, came in and said angrily: "Grandma, it isn't called sexual intercourse; it's called bunk beds. And Jimmy's Mom wants to talk to you."

* * * * *

I would like to share an experience with all of you. It has to do with drinking and driving. I was out for dinner with a few friends, and let's admit it, I had a bit too much wine to drink. So I did something I'd never done before. Believe it or not, I took a bus home! Yes, a bus! I arrived home safely and without incident. This was really a surprise, since I have never driven a bus before.

* * * * *

If a barber makes a mistake, it's a new style. If an executive makes a mistake, it's a new venture. If parents make a mistake, it's a new generation. If an engineer makes a mistake, it's a new invention. If a tailor makes a mistake, it's a new fashion. If a teacher makes a mistake, it's a new theory. But if an employee makes a mistake, it's a MISTAKE!

A lawyer is standing on a ticket line. Suddenly, he feels a pair of hands kneading his shoulders, neck, and back.

The lawyer turns around. "What the hell do you think you're doing?"

"I'm a chiropractor, and I'm just keeping in practice while I'm waiting in line."

"Well, I'm a lawyer, and you don't see me screwing the guy in front of me, do you?"

* * * * *

I was at the airport, checking in at the gate, when the airport employee asked, "Has anyone put anything into your luggage without your knowledge?"

I said, "If it was without my knowledge, how would I know?"

He smiled and nodded. "That's why we ask."

* * * * *

The stoplight on the corner buzzes when it is safe to cross the street. I was crossing with a rather dunderheaded co-worker of mine; and he asked if I knew what the buzzer was for. I explained that it signals to blind people when the light is red.

Appalled, he said, "What on earth are blind people doing, driving?"

* * * * *

CALLER: Can I please speak with Mr. Hunt? ME: I'm sorry, he's on vacation. CALLER: I'll hold.

At a goodbye lunch for an old, dear co-worker who had been downsized, our manager spoke up and said, "This is fun. We should have lunch like this more often." The stunned silence was deafening.

* * * * *

My friend Dan hates all this terrorist business. He says, "I used to love the good old days when you could look at an unattended bag on a train or a bus and think to yourself, "I'm going to take that."

* * * * *

Man in a hot-air balloon is lost over Mississippi. He looks down and sees a farmer in the fields and shouts down to him: "Where am I?" The farmer squints up at him and shouts back: "You're in that basket!"

* * * * *

The Englishman had just come out of the shop with a large meat and potato pie, fish and chips, mushy peas and a jumbo sausage.

A poor homeless man sitting against the shop wall said, "I've not eaten for two days."

Said the man: "I wish I had your willpower."

* * * * *

Man tells doctor: "My hands shake terribly." "Do you drink much?" "No, most of it spills."

A man was in a terrible accident which mangled and tore his penis quite badly. His doctor assured him that the latest in plastic surgery could give him back his manhood, but insurance wouldn't cover it.

The doctor said it would be $3,500 for "small, $6,500 for "medium" and $15,000 for "large."

The man was sure he'd want medium or large, but the doctor urged him to talk it over with his wife before he made any final decision.

The patient picked up his cell phone to call his wife and the doctor left the room. When he returned, he found the man looking dejected.

"Well, what have the two of you decided?" he asked.

Said the man: "She'd rather remodel the kitchen."

* * * * *

A husband and wife had a bitter quarrel on the day of their 40th anniversary.

The husband yelled, "When you die, I'm getting you a headstone that reads, "Here Lies My Wife–Cold as Ever!"

"Oh, yeah?" she replies. "Well, when you die, I'm getting you a headstone that reads, "Here Lies my Husband–Stiff at Last!"

* * * * *

A transvestite is he who likes to eat, drink, and be Mary.

A man wrote to a hotel in Chicago where he was planning to stay, asking if he might bring his dog with him. "He is well-behaved and well-groomed. Will you permit him to stay with me in my room?"

Replied the hotel owner: "In 30 years, I've never had a dog steal bedclothes, towels, silverware, or pictures off the wall. I've never had to kick a dog out for being drunk and disorderly. AndI've never had a dog skip out on a bill. So, yes, your dog is welcome at my hotel. And if your dog will vouch for you, you're welcome to stay, too."

* * * * *

A couple of years ago, at Kennedy Airport, an individual, later discovered to be a public school teacher was arrested trying to board a flight while in possession of a ruler, a protractor, a square, a slide rule and a calculator. It was believed that this man is a member of the notorious Al-Gebra movement and he was charged with carrying weapons of math destruction.

Said the Attorney General: "Al-Gebra is fearsome. They desire average solutions by means and extremes and sometime go off on tangents in search of an absolute value. They can't be trusted."

When asked to comment on the situation, President Bush said, "If God had wanted us to have better weapons of math destruction, he'd have given us more fingers and toes."

A Tennessee State Trooper pulled over a pickup on I-65.

"Got any I.D.?" the Trooper asked.

The driver replied: "'Bout whut?"

* * * * *

In Texas, the Sheriff pulled up next to the guy unloading garbage into a ditch.

"Why are you dumping garbage there?" demanded the Sheriff. "Don't you see that sign there?"

"Yep," replied the man. "That's why I'm dumping it here, 'cause it says, 'Fine for dumping garbage.'"

* * * * *

Patrick was visiting New York City. He was patiently waiting and watching the traffic cop at the crossing. The cop would stop the traffic and yell: "Okay, pedestrians." After they'd crossed, he'd let the traffic continue. After the tenth time this happened, Patrick went over to him and said, "Is it not about time ye let the Catholics across?"

* * * * *

My wife was hinting about what she wanted for our upcoming anniversary. She said, "I have in mind something shiny that goes from 0 to 150 in about three seconds." I bought her a bathroom scale. And that's when the fight started.

Here's how to achieve inner peace and calm. My doctor said to have inner peace, we should always finish the things we started. So I looked around my house to find the things I'd started and hadn't finished.

I finished off a bottle of merlot, a bottle of chardonnay, a bodle of beaileys, abutle of wum, the mainder of valiuminum scriptins an a box a chocletz ? Yu haf no idr how fablus I feel rite now.

sned this to all who need inner piss, an telum u luvum.

* * * * *

I rear-ended a car this morning....the start of a really bad day!

When the driver got out of the other car, I saw he was a little person, a dwarf.

He looked up at me and said, "I am NOT happy."

So I said, "Well, which one ARE you?"

That's how the fight started.

* * * * *

A senior citizen in Louisiana was overheard saying, "When the end of the world comes, I hope I'm in Louisiana."

"You hope to be in Louisiana for the end of the world? Why?"

"Because everything happens in Louisiana 20 years later than anywhere else in the world."

Father Murphy walks into a pub in Donegal, and asks the first man he meets, "Do you want to go to heaven?" "Yes, Father, of course I do."

"Then stand there against the wall.

The priest asks a second man the same question, and a third. Soon, they're standing against the wall.

Then Father Murphy walks up to O'Leary and asks, "Do you want to go to heaven?"

O'Leary says, "No, Father, I don't."

Father Murphy says, "I find this hard to believe. Do you mean to say that when you die you don't want to go to heaven?"

O'Leary says, "Oh. When I die, yes. I thought you were getting a group together to go right now."

* * * * *

The young man from Mississippi came running into the store, panting. Breathlessly, he said to his friend, "Bubba! Come quick! Somebody just stole your pickup truck from the parking lot!"

Bubba said, "Did you see who it was??

His friend answered, "It happened too fast for me to see the driver, but I got the license plate number!"

* * * * *

When I worked in tech support, I got a call asking when the call center was open. "We're open 24/7." "Is that Eastern or Pacific time?" he asked.

How many Californians does it take to change a lightbulb?
Six. One to turn the bulb, one for support, and four to relate to the experience.

How many psychiatrists does it take?
Only one, but the bulb has got to really want to change.

How many feminists does it take?
That's not funny!

How many software people does it take?
None. That's a hardware problem.

How many Calvinists does it take?
None. God has predestined when the light will come on.

How many Baptists?
CHANGE? But we never change!

How many Pentecostals?
Ten. One to change the bulb and nine to pray against the spirit of darkness.

How many TV evangelists?
One. But for the light to continue, send in your donation, thankyouverymuch!

PREGNANCY Q AND A

Q: Should I have a baby after 35?
A: No, 35 children are quite enough.

Q: What's the most reliable method to determine the baby's sex?
A: Childbirth

Q: My childbirth instructor says I won't feel pain during labor, only pressure. Is she right?
A: Yes, in the same way a tornado might be called an unruly air current.

Q: Is there anything I should avoid while recovering from childbirth?
A: Yes. Pregnancy.

Q: Do I have to have a baby shower?
A: Not if you change the baby's diaper very quickly.

Q: Our baby was born last week. When will my wife begin to feel and act normal again?
A: When the kids are in college.

MARRIAGE: Marriage is like a deck of cards.

In the beginning, all you need is two hearts and a diamond.

By the end, you wish you had a freakin' club and a spade.

There I was sitting at the bar staring at my drink when a large trouble-making biker steps up next to me, grabs my drink and gulps it down in one swig.

"Well, whatcha gonna do about it?" he says, as I burst into tears.

"Come on, man," says the biker. "I didn't think you'd CRY. I can't stand to see a man crying."

"This is the worst day of my life," I tell him. "I'm a complete failure. I was late to a meeting and the boss fired me. When I went to the parking lot, I found my car had been stolen an d I don't have any insurance. I left my wallet in the car I took home. I found my wife in bed with the gardener and then my dog bit me.

"So I came to this bar to work up the courage to put an end to it all. I bought a drink, I dropped a capsule of poison in and sat here watching it dissolve.

"Then you showed up and had to drink the whole thing!"

* * * * *

"The budget should be balanced, the Treasury should be refilled, public debt should be reduced, the arrogance of officialdom should be tempered and controlled, and assistance to foreign lands should be curtailed lest Rome becomes bankrupt. People must once again learn to work, instead of living on public assistance."

Cicero wrote that in 55 B.C.E. So what have we learned since then? Evidently...NOTHING.

Many times when I am troubled or confused, I find comfort in sitting in my backyard, drinking a vodka and cranberry and having a quiet conversation with Jesus.

This happened to me again after a particularly difficult day. I said, "Jesus, why do I work so hard?"

And I heard the reply. "Men find many ways to demonstrate the love they have to their family. You work hard to have a peaceful, beautiful place for your family and friends to gather."

I said, "I thought that money was the root of all evil."

The reply was, "No, the LOVE of money is the root of all evil. Money is a tool; it can be used for good or for bad."

I was starting to feel better, but I still had one burning question: "Jesus," I said, "What is the meaning of life? Why am I here?"

And Jesus replied: "That is a question many men ask. The answer is in your heart and is different for everyone. And I would love to chat with you some more, Senor, but now, I have to finish your lawn."

* * * * *

They keep telling us we should get in touch with our bodies. Mine isn't all that communicative, but I heard from it Tuesday morning when I proposed that we go to the 9:00 o'clock class in vigorous toning with resistance. Clear as a bell, my body said, "Listen, bitch, do it and you die!" -Molly Ivins

Sad news from Louisiana: It is with a heavy heart that I pass this on to you; but there will beno more Boudreaux and Thibodeaux jokes. Last week, Thibodeaux suddenly passed away. Boudreaux was grief-stricken at the loss of his lifelong friend. Being a fisherman and trapper, it was Thibodeaux's wish to be buried at sea. Alas, proof Boudreaux drowned attempting to dig the grave.

* * * * *

Ignorance is bliss. But it'll never replace sex.

* * * * *

The wife of fifty years tells her husband, "Go to the deli and bring me a hot pastrami on rye. Can you remember that?" He says, "Of course I can!"

A while later, he returns. "Here's your bagel."

She says, "So where's the cream cheese?"

* * * * *

An oyster and a lobster are making love. When a shrimp swims over, the lobster leaves.

Shrimp: How can you have sex with that lobster? He's so ugly... and those claws! Yuck!"

Oyster: "You don't understand. He has great moves. When he touches me on my chest, it's heaven, when he caresses my thighs, it's electric. And when he nibbles at my neck...Oh, God! My pearls! Where are my pearls?"

My new supermarket is really wonderful. The produce section smells like fruits and vegetables. When you go to the dairy department, you smell grass, hear a cow mooing, and the smell of butter on toast. Pass the meat case and you smell charcoal grilled steaks with onions. When you approach the egg case, you hear hens clucking and cackling, and the air is filled with the pleasing scent of bacon and eggs fying. The bakery department features the tantalizing smell of fresh baked bread and cookies.

I don't buy toilet paper there anymore.

* * * * *

Two young businessmen in Florida were sitting down for a break in their soon-to-be-opened department store. As yet, the store wasn't ready, although it had been painted and the shelves and racks were up. One of the businessmen said to the other, "I'll bet that any minute now, some senior citizen is going to put his face in the window, and ask what we're selling."

Sure enough, a moment later, a curious senior gentleman walked up to the window, looked around, and rapped on the glass. In a loud voice, he inquired: "What are you selling here?"

On of the men said, "Assholes."

Without missing a beat, the old timer said, "You must be doing well. Only two left."

Seniors: don't mess with them!

ACTUAL COURTROOM Q AND A:

Q: Did you see my client flee the scene?
A: No, sir, I didn't. But subsequently I observed someone running several blocks away who matched the description of the offender.
Q: Who provided you with the description?
A: The officer who responded to the scene.
Q: A fellow officer of yours provided the description of this so-called offender. Do you trust this fellow officer?
A: Yes, sir, with my life.
Q: With your life...hmmm. Let me then ask you this, officer. Do you have a room where you change your clothes in preparation for the day's duties?
A: Yes, sir, we do.
Q: And you have a locker in that room?
A: Yes, sir.
Q: And is there a lock on that locker?
A: Yes, sir, there is.
Q: Why is it, officer, that if you trust your fellow officers with you life, that you find it necessary to lock your locker in a room you share with those same officers?
A: You see, sir, we share the building with the court complex. And sometimes, lawyers have been known to walk through that room.

* * * * *